"*Solidarity Unionism* is an essential text for all rank-and-file workers as well as labor activists. Beautifully succinct, it outlines how CIO unions grew into an ineffectual model for rank-and-file empowerment, and provides examples of how alternative labor organizations have flourished in the wake of this. Lynd illustrates to a new generation of workers that we do have alternatives, and his call for a qualitatively different kind of labor organization gives us an ideological and strategic framework that we can apply in our day-to-day struggles on the shop floor."

 —Diane Krauthamer, *Industrial Worker*

"Brother Staughton Lynd continues to offer an informed, critical voice and many important ideas for today's labor movement. Anyone fighting for a better world for working people will be glad to read this revised edition of *Solidarity Unionism*, and to pass it on to students, friends, and fellow workers."

 —Michael Honey, Haley Professor of Humanities,
  University of Washington–Tacoma, and author of
  Going Down Jericho Road

"*Solidarity Unionism* is based in a vision of genuine democracy. It's accessibly written and rich in practical examples. I've used it successfully in study groups and labor education courses both to draw out and learn from participants' own experiences and to plan our next steps in struggles. Challenging some of what are conventionally thought of as 'wins' (e.g., dues checkoff or signed contracts), the book impels the kind of strategic thinking otherwise lacking in most of labor and the Left."

—Norm Diamond, former president of Pacific Northwest Labor College and coauthor of *The Power in Our Hands*

"Staughton Lynd's *Solidarity Unionism* mines his decades of labor activism and a century of American workers' struggles to shine a beacon on an alternative path that replaces top-down labor organization with local autonomy and community-level networking. Before you despair of reasserting workers' rights and power, read *Solidarity Unionism*!"

—Jeremy Brecher, Labor Network for Sustainability, author of *Strike!*

"In *Solidarity Unionism*, workers are protagonists, not spectators, and that makes all the difference in the world. Staughton Lynd's ideas will be at the heart of the next mass worker rising."

—Daniel Gross, executive director of Brandworkers and cofounder of IWW Starbucks Workers Union

Solidarity Unionism

Rebuilding the Labor Movement from Below

Second Edition

Staughton Lynd

With illustrations by Mike Konopacki

Introduction by Immanuel Ness

Solidarity Unionism: Rebuilding the Labor Movement from Below
Second Edition
© 2015 Staughton Lynd
This edition © 2015 PM Press

ISBN: 978-1-62963-096-0
LCCN: 2015930870

Cover design by John Yates/stealworks.com
Cover artwork by Mike Konopacki
Interior design by Jonathan Rowland

PM Press
PO Box 23912
Oakland, CA 94623
www.pmpress.org

10 9 8 7 6 5 4 3 2 1

Printed by the Employee Owners of Thomson-Shore in Dexter, Michigan.
www.thomsonshore.com

Contents

Introduction

STAUGHTON LYND'S BOOK WAS MEANT TO GIVE HOPE TO rank-and-file workers in the early 1990s battered by decades of continuous assault by capital and the state.

From the 1970s to the 1990s, business had emerged triumphant over established unions in the United States and throughout the world. Organized labor and academic liberals were mesmerized by the image of a strong welfare state and robust political parties as defenders of working-class interests against an ascendant capitalist class. Three years after this book was published, beleaguered leaders of the AFL-CIO placed the blame for the decline of organized labor in the United States on its own ossified leadership. They were convinced that all that was necessary to rebuild organized labor was to replace the existing union leadership with smart progressives skilled at recruiting workers. Union leaders ignored and dismissed their own members who were waging a prolonged insurgency for a voice in their organizations. Today, after twenty more years of political and organizational gimmickry, established unions have seen membership decline even further and remain impervious to rank-and-file participation in their organizations.

Now more than ever, this book remains prescient for working people.

For a couple of decades Staughton and I have, without end, discussed building and strengthening authentic unions forged in solidarity. What does it mean to have a workers' union based on solidarity? Must solidarity unions remain independent of existing unions? Are workers' centers the answer to promoting rank-and-file activity? How do we foster and strengthen solidarity unions across the United States and the world?

Staughton, among the leading historians of our time, asked all of us to look for real examples rather than abstract concepts that may have fit more neatly into our worldviews. In this book he takes succor in the lived experiences of courageous workers in Youngstown, Ohio, and beyond, recognizing that they have a common interest in solidarity, as he and his wife Alice showed in their book *Rank and File*.

In *Solidarity Unionism*, Staughton refers to the notion of "parallel labor unions" of rank-and-file workers. Parallel unions are committees of workers on the shop floor, and within the communities where their members live and work. They build solidarity through common action. They have been fundamental to the history and growth of working-class organizations in the United States and throughout the world.

When the official labor bodies put down workers, parallel unions like the Workers' Solidarity Club of Youngstown have come together outside of official union structures to defend workers' common interests. As Staughton shows in this book, these new structures are not new. They demonstrate that life exists outside of the entrenched bureaucratic unions that have bound and restricted worker self-activity since the formation of the CIO in the 1930s. They are the lifeblood of workers' organizations and what traditional unions have suppressed as they have sought to become third-party brokers between management and labor.

But I always put the question to Staughton: How do we build working-class organizations that are strong and lasting? The thesis of this book is that it is possible to have strong and lasting unions based on rank-and-file solidarity. We must look to examples drawn from the Industrial Workers of the World (IWW) and solidarity unions in the Global South. These workers in Africa, Asia, Latin America, and beyond are the most oppressed laborers in the world. They are employed in factories and mines at a fraction of the wages earned in North America, Japan, and Western Europe. Today, these workers exemplify the spirit of Solidarity Unionism as they struggle together for dignity and multinational capital, in league with state officials, seeks to marginalize, divide, and extract from them.[1]

The tragedy of traditional unions is that they have let us all down. As Staughton writes: "The existing trade unions may drop our grievances, compromise our just demands, and break our hearts, but we are not trying to destroy them." However, the assault on existing unions has also opened up

---

1. See Beverly Silver, *Forces of Labor: Workers' Movements and Globalization Since 1870* (New York: Cambridge University Press, 2003). Silver provides a persuasive examination and analysis of the historical significance of the workers' movements that are forming in the Global South in response to the growth of capitalist investment and industrialization.

a new front of worker activism that the capitalist class fears more than ever. Since most unions have signed on to laws and contracts that have given up workers' right to strike, young rank-and-file workers recognize that management-labor cooperation is the source of their oppression. They are engaging in direct action and mass strikes, and forming workers' assemblies, independent workers' committees and organizations. If this self-activity from below goes unheeded, traditional unions risk losing any relevancy to most workers.

After all the clamor by a new generation of labor leaders that they would rebuild the union movement, Staughton writes about these unions: "Far from prefiguring a new society, they are institutional dinosaurs resembling nothing so much as the corporations we are striving to replace." Unfortunately the existing labor unions have tainted the DNA of rank-and-file workers' organizations in North America, Europe, and beyond. Under labor law, union leaders have not challenged management's self-proclaimed prerogative under capitalism to move businesses to new locations at will.

With the growth of financialization, capital has expanded through the creation of new capital markets as David Harvey asserts:

> The tensions between competition and monopoly, between concentration and dispersal, between centralization and decentralization, between fixity and motion, between dynamism and inertia, between different scales of activity, all arise out of the molecular processes of endless capital

accumulation in space and time. . . . The aggregate effect is
. . . that capitalism perpetually seeks to create a geographi-
cal landscape to facilitate its activities at one point in time
only to have to destroy it and build a wholly different landscape at a later point in time to accommodate its perpetual
thirst for endless capital accumulation. Thus is the history
of creative destruction written into the landscape of the
actual historical geography of capital accumulation.[2]

The expansion of the urban industrial working class in
the Global South for forty years is contributing to the emergence of new organizational forms. For the last three decades
from 1980 to 2011, the share of industrial employment in
the global South expanded from just over 50 percent to 80
percent of the world's 3.27 million workers in the formal
sectors of the economy.[3] As finance capital seeks to avoid
traditional unions in the Global North and directs investment to nonunion or employer-dominated union enterprises
rank-and-file workers are forming new organizations to defend their collective interests. The global shift in production
to the South and the weakness and remoteness of established
unions to working people everywhere has contributed to

---

2. David Harvey, *The New Imperialism* (Oxford: Oxford University
Press, 2003), p. 101.
3. The World Bank, "World Development Indicators 2013," last
updated September 23, 2013. Note the data include European
workers in the former Soviet Bloc. See also John Bellamy Forster and
Robert W. McChesney, *The Endless Crisis: How Monopoly-Finance
Capital Produces Stagnation and Upheaval from the USA to China* (New
York: Monthly Review Press, 2012), pp. 127–28.

the rise of worker self-activity and solidarity unions in Asia, Africa, and Latin America (and China!).

Workers are forming new rank-and-file organizations throughout the world as the alternative to existing unions. In the last decade, autoworkers in India and mineworkers in South Africa are illustrative of the direction of working-class direct action and insurgency, taking the forms described in *Solidarity Unionism*.

India

While India is regarded by economists as a successful model for economic development, commentators neglect the country's linkages with investments that intensify inequality and exploitation of the vast majority. In India, independent rank-and-file workers' unions have arisen as foreign direct investment has eroded the power of traditional labor unions. Multinational companies demand strict subservience and impose intensified conditions on precarious workers. In response, new class-struggle unions are forming and expanding in India's industrial belts.

Workers employed at Maruti Suzuki (MSIL), India's largest manufacturer of automobiles, are engaging in rank-and-file unionism that is illustrative of what it means to practice Solidarity Unionism. MSIL produces about 1.2 million vehicles a year for the domestic and international market, and has been a center of new worker organizations.[4]

---

4. On state and societal relations in India, see Vivek Chibber, *Locked*

The company claims that its plant in Manesar, twenty-five miles southwest of New Delhi, produces cars faster than any in the world: one every forty-five seconds. This rapid assembling of automobiles is produced through introduction of high technology, low wages, a two-tier labor force, and the acceleration of the line. The policy contributes to worker productivity at MSIL, which is the most profitable unit of Suzuki Motor Corporation.

Wages and working conditions for full-time and contract workers at the Manesar plant are low even by Indian standards. Even for full-time workers, MSIL pegs pay to productivity rather than paying set wages. The company pays far less than other auto producers—barely enough for

in Place: State-Building and Late Industrialization in India (Princeton, NJ: Princeton University Press, 2006). For analysis of workers and the Indian labor movement, see Research Unit for Political Economy, "Behind the Present Wave of Unrest in the Labor Sector," *Aspects of India's Economy* 52, June 2012, http://rupe-india.org/52/auto.html; Jan Breman, "A Dualistic Labour System? A Critique of the Informal Sector Concept: I. The Informal Sector," *Economic and Political Weekly* 11, no. 48 (November 27, 1976), pp. 1870–76; Robin Hensman, *Workers, Unions, and Global Capitalism: Lessons from India* (New York: Columbia University Press, 2011); People's Union for Democratic Rights, *Driving Force: Labour Struggles and Violation of Rights in Maruti Suzuki India Limited* (New Delhi, India: 2013); *Workers Autonomy Strikes in India: Maruti Suzuki Strike at Manesar* (Brussels, Belgium: Kolektivne proti Kapitalu & Mouvement Communiste, #5, May 2012); *Merchants of Menace: The Repression of Workers in India's New Industrial Belt* (New York: International Commission for Labor Rights, 2013); Rakhi Segal, "'Manesar Workers Are the Villains': Truth or Prejudice?," *Economic & Political Weekly* 47, no. 31, August 4, 2012; http://www.epw.in/ejournal/show/1/_/2172?quicktabs_issues_tab=0&quicktabs_most_co mmented_read=0.

workers to meet basic necessities of life. Workers are deprived of break time, and typically work two hours overtime each day. Contract workers, who perform the same functions as permanent workers without job security or benefits, are 75 percent of the workforce. Since the state fails to enforce its own labor laws, autoworkers at Maruti Suzuki and other manufacturing plants in the major industrial belts are organizing independent unions to improve wages and conditions.

On Wednesday, July 18, 2012, two months after the workers founded the independent union Maruti Suzuki Workers Union (MSWU), the company dispatched bouncers into the plant to intimidate and attack rank-and-file activists. Mayhem followed. Workers fled. The human resources department was set on fire, leading to the asphyxiation of the only human resources manager who supported the new union. To place blame for the death on the workers—though they had already left the plant when the blaze was set—management enlisted the Haryana state police to hunt down and arrest hundreds of workers, seeking to charge them with murder.

Family members and friends in the community were detained and harassed into revealing the whereabouts of their worker relatives. Many were tortured at the hands of local police, and family members beaten. As I write in March 2014, the state continues to hold 147 MSWU rank-and-file activists in jail without charges or bail, while 66 others are in hiding. The workers face criminal charges of conspiracy, attempted murder, and murder—all based on little evidence. To create a compliant workforce, a month after the incident,

Maruti Suzuki permanently replaced all the workers, terminating 546 permanent and 1,800 contract workers.

Organizing against Capital and Government

From 2010 to the present, Maruti workers built local and national support for their struggle, resisting employer lockouts and conducting two sitdown strikes. They began organizing in early 2011 to challenge the tiered wage system and oppressive conditions. Workers sought to equalize wages and conditions between permanent and informal workers, who receive low wages and are regularly dismissed.

But multinational auto manufacturers have the unequivocal support of government authorities in fending off unions. Police arrest workers who mobilize; judges in the state courts keep them in jail. After an illegal lockout in 2011 Maruti Suzuki workers staged a thirty-three-day sitdown strike in August 2011, the third major worker agitation of the year at the Manesar plant.

The action ended in a compromise. But when permanent workers learned that casual workers would be dismissed, they began another sitdown inside the factory, while casual workers maintained their sit-in outside the plant gates. The workers sustained the sitdown even when management hired private security personnel, known as bouncers, to attack them. Through the resilience of the workers, all casual workers were reinstated. But the Indian federal and state governments are controlled by corporate interests opposed to independent unions. When MSWU requested the official registration of their fledgling union with the Haryana state Department of Labour in May 2012, MSIL management responded fiercely, initiating an unprecedented campaign of intimidation, terror, and violence with the active support of Haryana authorities and the complicity of the Indian government.

Despite intimidation, threats of violence, and dismissal, workers in India have rejected management's effort to impose company unions, demanding instead independent unions free of employer domination. MSWU is one of many independent unions proliferating in India, as the traditional unions decline quickly and as direct foreign investments expand throughout the country and profits are appropriated by multinationals in the Global North. North American, Western European, and East Asian corporations are investing in manufacturing and high technology in India on the condition that independent unions are suppressed, helping to ensure high profit margins. In particular, foreign companies thrive on a workforce comprised primarily of informal contract laborers who have no rights. Contract and temporary workers represent a majority of workers in India's manufacturing sector, keeping wages down for all.

The wage differential between permanent and contract workers ranges from a ratio of 4:1 to 5:1, jeopardizing a growing number of permanent jobs. The appearance of independent plant-level formations, unifying full-time and informal workers, is a direct consequence of opposition to traditional unions that have allowed multi-tier wage systems. While employers seek out young migrant recruits to replace seasoned workers, the Maruti Suzuki struggle demonstrates that newly proletarianized workers are carrying on resilient struggles unifying the working class throughout India, a remarkable development given the lack of any meaningful protection against dismissal.

South Africa

In recent years, South African workers have formed assemblies to express their rights, severely circumscribed by government and labor union authorities.[5] While the

5. For a history of mineworkers in South Africa, see Luli Callinicos, *A People's History of South Africa*, vol. 1 (Johannesburg: Raven Press, 1981). For an examination of the militant workers' movement in the 1980s that shaped the formation and the fierce independence of NUMSA, see Kelly Forest, *Metal That Will Not Bend: The National Union of Metalworkers of South Africa, 1980–1995* (Johannesburg: Witwatersrand University Press, 2011). For an account of the evolution of the South African labor movement in the post-apartheid era, see John Saul, "On Taming the Revolution: The South African Case," in Leo Panitch, Greg Albo, and Vivek Chibber, *Socialist Register 2013: The Question of Strategy* (London: Merlin Press, 2012), pp. 212–40. For an account of the South African mineworker insurgencies from 2009 to the present, including the wildcat strikes at Marikana, see Vishwas Satgar, "Beyond Marikana: The Post-Apartheid South African State," *Africa Spectrum* 47, no. 2–3 (2012), pp. 33–62; Patrick Bond, "The Marikana Movement Has Stunned Liberal South Africa," *Brave New World*, October 22, 2012; Peter Alexander, Thapelo Lekgowa, Botsang Minope, Luke Sinwell, Bongani Xezwi, *Marikana, Voices from South Africa's Mining Massacre* (London: Bookmarks, 2013); and Shawn Hattingh, "Exploding Anger: Workers' Struggles and Self-Organization in South Africa's Mining Industry," in Immanuel Ness, ed., *New Forms of Worker Organization: The Syndicalist and Autonomous Restoration of Class Struggle Unionism* (Oakland: PM Press, 2014).

post-apartheid era granted political rights to Black South Africans as citizens, the new government severely restricted economic rights among workers who waged strikes that helped bring an end to the system of racial oppression. The post-apartheid government that emerged sought to rein in the workers' struggles by creating a tripartite government in 1994 unifying the African National Congress (ANC), South African Communist Party (SACP), and the Confederation of South African Trade Unions (COSATU).

In 1995, South African labor law created an atmosphere of labor–management collaboration. The state's embrace of neoliberal capitalism is total, and accompanies an unequivocal decline in organized trade union power under an ANC government. That government has sought to channel spontaneous worker agitation and dissent against corporate management into a formal system of labor relations that regulates and contains rank-and-file direct action and strikes. The unwillingness of the state and organized labor seriously to address the rise of two-tier contract labor systems and declining wages has stimulated informal and migrant worker self-activity and unsanctioned mass action that is challenging the credibility of the government and trade union leaders.

Rather than giving a voice to rank-and-file workers in unions, the new law restricted strikes and concerted action outside collective bargaining agreements and expanded the use of contractors who hired informal workers at a fraction of the standard wages. Some COSATU union leaders maintained close ties to the government and often served as corporate puppets to the government and multinational capital. Most tarnished is the National Union of Mineworkers (NUM), which was deemed by an independent panel to be complicit in the Marikana Massacre and in other atrocities by the South African police against miners and their families.

Mineworker Wildcat Strikes and the Marikana Massacre

The Marikana Massacre occurred on August 16, 2012, when an elite unit of the South African State Police fired on hundreds of mineworkers who were on a wildcat strike, killing thirty-four and wounding seventy-eight. Marikana was the most deadly massacre since the Sharpeville Massacre of March 21, 1960, by the apartheid-dominated government and it called attention to widening inequality and growing poverty in the post-apartheid era. With the support of the South African government, Lonmin Platinum, and, distressingly, leaders of the National Union of Mineworkers, the state police were determined to remove hundreds of striking workers who had assembled on a mountain ridge near the Lonmin mines. Two years later, a government commission found that the state police deliberately killed and wounded the striking workers who had encamped on the mountain, demanding that the platinum producer increase wages for both permanent workers and informal contract rockdrillers who mine the ore deep underground. The workers at Marikana mobilized a popular assembly to demand higher wages and improved living conditions at Lonmin and throughout the mining belt of South Africa's North West province. The wildcat strike and massacre signified to all South Africans the resilience of rank-and-file mineworkers mobilized in solidarity against a multinational corporation, the state security apparatus, and an unresponsive union.

Marikana has been the defining moment in the mineworker struggle for autonomy and dignity. Marikana demonstrated that not only were workers fired, assaulted, and jailed, but that police seem able freely to kill workers who challenge the status quo with the support of NUM, which has come to resemble a company-dominated union.

The Marikana workers' struggle of 2012 and the growth of militancy throughout the mining sector grew out of the rise in mineworker militancy in the Bushveld in 2009. Organization came about rapidly and unpredictably as workers lost confidence in formal state institutions and labor organizations that failed to legitimize and represent their interests. Instead workers conveyed their demands through parallel rank-and-file workers' organizations and the formation of workers' assemblies. A wave of unauthorized strikes forced the South African mining industry to grant significant wage concessions to workers in the mining-rich Merensky mining belt of North West province in South Africa.

The formation of an independent union at Marikana indicates that mineworkers viewed NUM suspiciously as aligned with management. The appeal of the African Miners and Construction Union (AMCU) to platinum mineworkers owed more to a profound suspicion of NUM than to an authentic loyalty to the AMCU. Marikana rank-and-file workers distinguished themselves from the membership of the two mine unions. Identification with AMCU did not demonstrate unqualified support from Marikana workers, but a tactical alliance with a recognized union willing to advance rank-and-file objectives designed to achieve dignity on the job. As became clear in subsequent testimony before the Marikana Commission of Inquiry, strikers were comprised of both NUM and AMCU members and their loyalty was not to either union but to their nameless rank-and-file parallel workers' organization. They were determined to remain on the *koppie* (a South African hillock) come what may until management consented to their wage demand. Workers organized independently of either union to triple minimum monthly wages from about US$400 to $1,150 and continued to demand pay raises through a seven-week strike from February to March 2014 (ongoing as I write).

Arrayed in opposition to the insurgent working-class movement that has emerged in the mining industry, in addition to multinational capital and compliant bureaucratic trade unions closely aligned to the South African state, is a violent well-armed state system of repression. The repressive apparatus is institutionalized in the labor laws that criminalize workers who dare to challenge a legal system organized to defend capital against labor. Marikana displays that when an insurgent workers' movement effectively mobilizes to defy the validity of hegemonic laws that support the power of capital, the post-apartheid South African government will readily unleash its state security forces to destroy and oblit-erate all dissent. Marikana also demonstrates that South African workers who are deprived of legitimate labor repre-sentation will, even when facing injury and death, resist the state-capitalist system in order to advance their collective rights. Most importantly, the South African mineworkers have demonstrated that they can gain power through creat-ing and controlling their own unions rather than submitting to the dictates of union bureaucrats.

Conclusion

These two examples (which could be multiplied by reference to China, Indonesia, Mexico, Nigeria, Eastern Europe, and elsewhere) demonstrate that the only path to worker democ-racy and power is through solidarity unions that are formed directly by workers on the job. Staughton Lynd's concept of parallel unionism is both the means and end to contesting hierarchical unions that are cut off from members and estab-lishing broader working-class power. Workers mobilized in solidarity recall the principle "We Are All Leaders," an old IWW slogan that is also the title of a collection of essays edited by Staughton. The words recognize that workers are stronger making decisions in struggle together rather than through detached leaders.

Solidarity Unionism is a timeless book that warns us that if we rely on competent, smart professionals to run our union movement, it will lead to ruin. As academics suggest new directions for existing unions, Staughton proposes that if we

clear away the debris of the burned-over forest we will find
a new and stronger movement blooming underneath.

Solidarity Unionism is fundamental to Staughton Lynd's
lifelong project to authenticate, support, and work with
rank-and-file workers' organizations that are forming in the
United States and throughout the world. While many academics lament the decline of traditional unions, Staughton
takes succor in the blossoming of rank-and-file worker organizations throughout the world that are countering rapacious
capitalists and those comfortable labor leaders that think they
know more about work and struggle than their own members.
If we apply a new measure of workers' power that is deeply
rooted in gatherings of workers and communities, the bleak
and static perspective about the sorry state of labor today por-
trayed by most labor scholars becomes bright and dynamic.

To secure the gains of solidarity unions, Staughton has
proposed parallel bodies of workers who share the principles
of rank-and-file solidarity and can coordinate the activities
of local workers' assemblies. However imperfect and unfa-
miliar, we are beginning to see the emergence of parallel
coordinating bodies in locations such as India and South
Africa to provide crucial generalized and organized support
for local rank-and-file struggles.

In *Solidarity Unionism*, Lynd is pursuing a tradition that
workers understand but labor leaders reject. After so many
failures, it is time to frankly recognize that the century-old
system of recognition of a single union as exclusive collective
bargaining agent was fatally flawed from the beginning and
doesn't work for most workers.

I have focused on new labor organizations forming outside of the United States, where most of the workers of the world toil. They are setting examples for those, like Staughton and I, who can speak about solidarity without the threat of imprisonment or fear of death. If workers in the poor countries of the Global South are willing to go out on the line and risk their lives because their co-workers are earning a fraction of their wages, I ask myself why I cannot do the same for adjunct faculty members in my own university who make up the exploited majority of all faculty in the academy and work for a fraction of the full-time wage.

Factory workers in India and mineworkers in South Africa should be an inspiration to all of us who care about building a strong rank-and-file workers' movement in the United States and the Global North. For more than twenty years *Solidarity Unionism* and Staughton Lynd have represented to me what it means to be human and what is important in life. If we can't work together, even in adversity, we remain pawns of a destructive and invasive capitalist system that controls existing working-class organizations through existing unions. If we are to live with dignity, we must collectively resist. Staughton tells us in *Solidarity Unionism* how workers in Ohio have advanced solidarity unionism for our own dignity. This book is not a prescription but reveals the lived experience of working people continuously taking risks for the common good.

—Immanuel Ness

A Word to the Reader

What follows began as a talk I gave at a Conference on Workers' Self-Organization in Minneapolis in May 1990. A first edition was published in 1992. Coming back to it more than twenty years later, I have not changed the basic argument in any way. As I reviewed the text for this second edition, however, it seemed essential to add a few words. Since the early 1990s, the catastrophic decline in the percentage of workers in the United States who are members of unions has continued. But there has also been a revival and more widespread exploration of the "solidarity unionism" that is front and center in these pages. Of course it is perilous to predict the future. Still, twenty or even ten years ago one would not have expected that major unions like the United Food and Commercial Workers (UFCW) or Service Employees International Union (SEIU) would today be sponsoring campaigns among low-wage workers that ostensibly seek not to achieve exclusive bargaining status but to obtain immediate changes in particular conditions of employment through direct action.

I have added a few footnotes and supplemented others in order to recognize additional evidence for the ideas expressed in the first edition. And finally, I wish once again to emphasize that the core of what is set forth here derives from the vision and practice of a number of workers whom I am privileged to have known: John Sargent, first president of the local union at Inland Steel; the three "union maids," Katherine Hyndman, Vicki Starr (a.k.a. Stella Nowicki), and Sylvia Woods; Marty Glaberman and Stan Weir, lonely prophets; and Ed Mann, sometime president of Local 1462, United Steelworkers of America, and later a founding brother of the Workers' Solidarity Club of Youngstown and member of the Industrial Workers of the World (IWW).

I hope that this little book will be read by labor historians, by lawyers and law students active in the labor movement, but also and especially, by rank-and-file workers. For this last group of readers, in particular, I want to say two things by way of introduction.

First, if your experience is like mine, you have probably been attacked by trade union officers and staffers. You have been called a "dissident" and a "union basher." You have been accused of seeking to destroy existing unions, of dual unionism, of being anti-union.

We can try to rebut these attacks. We can say that the main enemy is, and always will be, the profit-seeking corporation, not the union. We can add that if, contrary to our expectations, the existing trade unions can democratize and renew themselves, and become a mighty force for social change, we will be glad to be proven wrong. The existing trade unions may drop our grievances, compromise our just demands, and break our hearts, but we are not trying to destroy them.

What we are trying to do, I think, is to build something new: a labor organization of a different kind. And in my opinion, the best way to respond to attacks is to continue that building, to show its usefulness in responding to problems, to demonstrate its attractiveness to our fellow workers.

How may this new kind of labor organization best be described?

To begin with, it must be democratic. Trade unions are among the most undemocratic institutions in the United States. Far from prefiguring a new society, they are institutional dinosaurs, resembling nothing so much as the corporations we are striving to replace. I used to say that trade unions in the United States were one-party governments like the government of the Soviet Union. Today I would say that there may have been more democracy in the Soviet Union than in many trade unions in the United States.

Democracy means, at a minimum, the freedom to criticize frankly and fully. Union bureaucrats have a tendency to view criticism as treason. But rank-and-file members must be able to criticize, not just the policies of incumbent union officers, but the structural shortcomings of the labor movement. For instance, CIO contracts have always contained no-strike and management prerogative clauses, but if we think (as I do) that these clauses are wrong and should be abolished, we should be free to say so.

As part of building more democratic labor organizations, we must be able to question the whole idea of unions as legal monopolies. In England, Spain, or Poland, to the best of my knowledge, the workers in a particular plant or office elect a workplace committee. The committee may be wholly made up of members of one union, or may include members of different unions, in proportion to the strength of those unions in that place of work, and bargains for the workplace as a whole until the next workplace elections. We should consider this system. We should also question whether we wish to require workers to belong to a union whether they want to or not, and whether it might not be better to have stewards collect dues on the shop floor, rather than have the employer deduct dues from everybody's paychecks.

The new committees and networks that we build will be based on solidarity as well as democracy. The ethic of solidarity, the idea that "an injury to one is an injury to all," is the best and most important thing about the labor movement. I once tried to describe it this way:

> The well-being of the individual and the well-being of the group are not experienced as antagonistic. Justice Sandra Day O'Connor has written that "the concepts of individual action for personal gain and 'concerted activity' are intuitively incompatible."[1] This is the view from the outside, the view of someone who has not experienced the wage worker's elemental need for the support of other workers. Learned Hand came much closer to the reality in a passage [written during the early days of the CIO]:
>
> "When all other workmen in a shop make common cause with a fellow workman over his separate grievance,

---

1. NLRB v. City Disposal Systems, 465 U.S. 822 (1984).

and go out on strike in his support, they engage in a 'concerted activity' for 'mutual aid or protection,' although the
aggrieved workman is the only one of them who has any
immediate stake in the outcome. The rest know that by
their action each one of them assures himself, in case his
turn ever comes, of the support of the one who they are all
then helping; and the solidarity so established is 'mutual
aid' in the most literal sense, as nobody doubts. So too
of those engaging in a 'sympathetic strike,' or secondary
boycott; the immediate quarrel does not itself concern
them, but by extending the number of those who will
make the enemy of one the enemy of all, the power of
each is vastly increased."[2]

I have heard a rank-and-file steelworker use almost
identical language in trying to persuade fellow workers
to support each other's grievances. What is counterintui-
tive to Justice O'Connor is the common sense of those
engaged in the struggle.

But the group of those who work together—the
informal work group, the department, the local union,
the class—is often experienced as a reality in itself. Thus,
Hand's rationale misses something crucial to the right to
engage in concerted activity. I do not scratch your back
only because one day I may need you to scratch mine.
Labor solidarity is more than an updated version of the
social contract, through which each individual undertakes

---

2. NLRB v. Peter Cailler Kohler Swiss Chocolates Co., 130 F.2d 503
(2d Cir. 1942).

to assist others for the advancement of his or her own interest.

In a family, when I as son, husband, or father, express love toward you, I do not do so in order to assure myself of love in return. I do not help my son in order to be able to claim assistance from him when I am old; I do it because he and I are in the world together, we are one flesh. Similarly in a workplace, persons who work together form families-at-work. When you and I are working together, and the foreman suddenly discharges you, and I find myself putting down my tools or stopping my machine before I have had time to think—why do I do this? Is it not because, as I actually experience the event, your discharge does not happen only to you but also happens to us?[3]

Working people believe in solidarity, not because they are better than other people, but because the power of the boss forces workers to reach out to each other for help. Because of the vision and practice of solidarity, the labor movement with all its shortcomings does prefigure a new kind of society within the shell of the old. And by building organizations based on solidarity, rather than on bureaucratic chain-of-command, we build organizations that by their very existence help to bring a new kind of society into being.

---

3. Staughton Lynd, "Communal Rights," *Texas Law Review* 62, no. 8 (May 1984), pp. 1426–27. Section 7 of the National Labor Relations Act protects the right to engage in concerted activity for the purpose of mutual aid or protection.

The second thing I want to say by way of introduction is that the basic ideas laid out in this little book are ideas that I share with many other people. In fact, most of the ideas in the book are ideas that I first heard from other people, five or ten years older than myself, who themselves came to these conclusions from personal experience in steel mills, automobile assembly plants, or other places of work.

For example, I first encountered the concept that CIO unions function as cops for the boss (especially in enforcing the no-strike clause) in a pamphlet by Marty Glaberman. Marty is an autoworker from Detroit. His experience goes back to the struggle against the no-strike clause during World War II, which he describes in a book called *Wartime Strikes: The Struggle Against the No-Strike Pledge in the UAW During World War II*. Then I heard the same thing from John Sargent, a steelworker who was the first president of Local 1010, United Steelworkers of America, at Inland Steel in East Chicago, Indiana. John summed up his four terms as local union president and a lifetime of serving the rank and file in a talk at a forum on "Labor History from the Viewpoint of the Rank and File" in 1970. He said then:

> The union has become a watchdog for the company. The local union has become the police force for the contracts made by the international union. If a local union tries to reject a contract in the Steelworkers Union, the contract is put into effect and the local union acts as the police to see that the men live up to the contract, even if

it is rejected by the entire committee [of the local union] which negotiates the contract.

. . . The government and the employers have learned how to adopt, co-opt, and engulf the union and make it a part of the establishment. And in making it part of the establishment they took the guts, the militancy, and the fight out of the people who work for a living.

John's talk can be read in a book edited by my wife Alice and myself, *Rank and File: Personal Histories of Working-Class Organizers*, eds. Alice and Staughton Lynd (updated edition; Chicago: Haymarket Books, 2011).

Stan Weir is another worker-writer who has influenced me and many others. Stan worked as a merchant seaman during World War II, and after the war, as an autoworker, teamster, and longshoreman. Among his distinctive ideas are: first, that the real power in the shop is in the informal group of people who work next to each other; second, that one way a worker can recognize how few his or her rights are is to compare the rights enjoyed by citizens outside the shop with the slimmer bundle of rights they have as workers once they punch in. Stan describes how he arrived at the concept of the "informal work group" in a personal history in *Rank and File*, the book already mentioned. He also started a small publishing venture, Singlejack Books, directed at publishing "writings about, or related to, work, written by the people who are doing it or have done it."

In Youngstown, where my wife and I have lived since 1976, the friend who has most influenced us is Ed Mann. Ed tells his story in an oral history, extracts from which appear as an appendix to this book. Some of the things Ed says there are:

> I think we've got too much contract. You hate to be the guy who talks about the good old days, but I think the IWW had a darn good idea when they said, "Well, we'll settle these things as they arise."
>
> I believe in direct action. Once a problem is put on paper and gets into the grievance procedure, you might as well kiss that paper goodbye. When the corporation started recognizing unions, they saw this. They co-opted the unions with the grievance procedure and the dues check-off. They quit dealing with the rank and file and started dealing with the people who wanted to be bosses like them, the union bosses.

Three times president of Local 1462, USWA, Ed has this to say about the vogue for "labor-management cooperation":

> The companies say they want workers to participate in the work process, in management. But they're not giving away any decision-making. The company's rights are very clear-cut and defined. You may be able to discuss how many parking places there will be in the parking lot, or what kind of pop will be in the pop machine. But when it comes to hiring, firing, disciplining, the rules of production and so on, you're not involved. They talk about "work teams." This is garbage. A work team tends to say, Hey, this guy isn't keeping up, let's get rid of him.

And finally this:

> The Wobblies say, Do away with the wage system. For a lot of people that's pretty hard to take. What the Wobblies mean is, you'll have what you need. The wage system has destroyed us. If I work hard I'll get ahead, but if I'm stronger than Jim over here, maybe I'll get the better job and Jim will be sweeping floors. But maybe Jim has four kids. The wage system is a very divisive thing. It's the only thing we have now, but it's very divisive. Maybe I'm just dreaming but I think there's a better way.

Chapter One

The View from Youngstown

THE IDEA OF REBUILDING THE LABOR MOVEMENT FROM BE-
low is, at first glance, overwhelming.

How do we deal with the fact that in a time when most of us are taking the merest first steps toward a new kind of labor movement, are necessarily working at a local level and in a very preliminary manner, are barely scratching the surface of the huge collective task of rethinking the assumptions on which the labor movement of the United States has proceeded at least since the 1930s, and in some respects since the 1880s—that just at this moment, when our work is properly so tentative and decentralized, capital has reorganized itself on a scale ever more far-flung and international? Doesn't the scope and power of capital's reorganization make our work, by contrast, almost grotesquely irrelevant? In suggesting that our work might be of some historical significance, who do we think we are kidding?

Like each of you, in approaching these questions I can only draw on my own experience. Let me quickly sketch the constituencies with whom I have worked, and how each of them views the future of the labor movement.

First, there are workers in non-union shops. Many of them worked in steel mills before the Youngstown mills shut

down in 1977–1980. Others are Blacks and women trying
to get a foothold in the labor force. Wages are typically very
little above state and federal minimum requirements of seven
to eight dollars an hour. Safety and health conditions are
atrocious. Yet these workers, who it would seem have every
reason to belong to unions, have been disillusioned by the
performance of big existing unions as they have experienced
it, or been told about it. Some have worked for a series of
companies that shut down or went bankrupt, while unions
stood by helpless. After one too many bankruptcy, plant
closing, or concession contract, the non-union workforce
in the Mahoning Valley is looking for something different than joining the Steelworkers, or the Teamsters, or the
autoworkers.

Secondly, there are persons who belong to existing
unions. In some cases the union headquarters is an hour
and a half away in Cleveland and meetings are never held
in Youngstown. In others the members do not even know
the name of the union to which they belong. The largest
unionized work force in the area is at General Motors
Lordstown. Workers there do know the name of their union.
In 1990, they also knew the name of the chairman of the
board, Roger Smith. That year GM gave each Lordstown
worker a profit-sharing check in the amount of fifty dollars. Workers at Ford and Chrysler received thousands of
dollars. Lordstown workers responded by circulating, first,
a picture of three fifty-dollar bills with Roger Smith's face
in the middle (instead of the picture of U.S. Grant), and
second, a leaflet ending with the words: "when . . . you really

feel you'd like to quit, don't come to me, I don't give a shit. ROGER SMITH."

Lordstown management then posted an Information Bulletin to the effect that Shop Rule #29 had been modified to cover "the making or publishing of malicious statements concerning any employee, the company or its products." The UAW locals have done nothing to challenge this shop rule, just as they did nothing to challenge the previous management practice of requiring employees to get leaflets approved by GM Labor Relations before passing them out in the plant parking lot.[1] The prevailing atmosphere is cynicism. The strongest single emotion is fear that the plant will close.

Finally, there are former members of unions who are retired or disabled. They may be the most alienated of all. For example, in 1990 LTV Steel had (nationwide) 13,800 active workers and 46,000 hourly retirees. Such retirees are no longer union members, do not vote for union officers, and have no voice in the negotiation or ratification of changes in their pension and medical benefits. In the 1990 LTV Steel contract, ratified by active workers alone, the average active worker received $7.25 in contract improvements for every $1 received by the average retiree. There was a company-wide retiree protest movement. Among its demands were that

---

1. The right of employees to pass out leaflets about their work in the company parking lot, without prior censorship, is protected by Section 7 of the National Labor Relations Act. When the union didn't do anything, Workers Against Toxic Chemical Hazards (WATCH) filed an NLRB charge and won.

retirees should have the right to vote on contract provisions changing their benefits.

All in all, the Youngstown scene is a bleak one. But the people just described have created some interesting organizations.

THE WORKERS' SOLIDARITY CLUB

The Workers' Solidarity Club can best be described as a parallel central labor union, to which rank-and-file workers, unemployed persons, and retirees could come when they needed help in their various struggles. Several members wrote this about the Club:

> We wanted a place where rank-and-file workers could go to get strike support without a lot of hassle and delay. We were disillusioned with big national unions that encourage their members to "pay your dues and leave the rest to us."
>
> We were called "rebels" and "dissidents" but we believed in solidarity, and we wanted a way to see each other regularly, share experiences, laugh at each other's jokes, and dream up plans to change the world.
>
> The Workers' Solidarity Club grew out of classes at the hall of Utility Workers Local 118, where the Club met. Local 118 had been through a long strike a couple of years earlier. There was a core of members who were eager to give tangible strike support to other workers on strike. In the fall of 1981, we held a series of discussions

at the hall on the topic, What has gone wrong with the labor movement? We talked about all kinds of things, for instance the new encyclical by the Pope called "On Human Labor." As the discussions drew to a close, we realized we didn't want to disband. We gave ourselves a name and started to meet monthly.

From the beginning, the Club was extremely informal. There were no officers except a treasurer. Two members got out a monthly notice describing what was expected to happen at the next meeting. Individuals volunteered (or were volunteered at the last moment) to chair particular meetings. If there was a speaker at a particular meeting, the person who invited the speaker was likely to become chairperson. There were no dues, but by passing the hat we raised hundreds of dollars for legal defense, publications, and travel expenses. We also raised money by selling bright red suspenders with the words "Workers' Solidarity" silk-screened in black. Beer at the end of every meeting, and annual picnics and Christmas parties, kept us cheerful.

Lots of Unions

The Workers' Solidarity Club was like a Wobbly "mixed local," or a local branch of Polish Solidarity, in that its members came from many different trades and unions. A typical leaflet was signed by twenty-five people. Of these, seventeen were current employees; they worked for Ohio Edison, Schwebel Baking Company, LTV Steel, and other enterprises. Six of the seventeen were stewards or local union officers. The remaining signers were retired or unemployed. The signers included current or past members of the Utility Workers, the Laborers, the Steelworkers, the Bakery Workers, the Teamsters, the Mineworkers, the Ohio Education Association, and the Amalgamated Clothing Workers.

Our first big action came in the summer of 1982. Service and maintenance workers at Trumbull Memorial Hospital in Warren, Ohio, organized in an AFSCME local, went on strike. Two members of the Club visited the picket line. The Club put out a series of leaflets. The leaflets appealed to strike-breakers not to cross the picket line. The first leaflet began: "THINK before you cross a picket line. Think before you take your neighbor's job."

The leaflet also invited members of other unions to rally every Wednesday afternoon in front of the hospital. The rallies grew larger and larger. People brought homemade banners and signs, and chanted slogans like: "Warren is a union town, we won't let you tear it down."

On October 13, 1982, there was a confrontation with the Warren police. Thirteen demonstrators were arrested, including three members of the Club: Ed Mann, retired president of a steelworkers' local; Greg Yarwick, a member of Local 118; and Ken Porter, laid off from a local cement company. The other arrestees entered agreed-on pleas for lesser offenses and paid a fine. Ed, Greg, and Ken pled not guilty, and were convicted of conspiracy to riot and resisting arrest. With the help of the ACLU they appealed to the Court of Appeals and Supreme Court of Ohio. In the end, not only were they acquitted, but the Club recovered $1,000 in court costs from the City of Warren.

As a result of all this mass activity, the AFSCME local survived the strike. After the strike, the Club conducted classes for sixty to eighty members of the AFSCME local at the hall of USWA Local 1375.

Other club activities included weekly picketing at the Bessemer Cement Company, which closed and cut off benefits only to reopen non-union under a different owner, and strike support for the Food and Commercial Workers. [After this article was written, the Club played a key role in supporting striking members of the Machinists at a Buick sales and service shop. Forbidden by a judge to engage in mass picketing, members of the Club invented the "honkathon": trade unionists from all over the Valley drove slowly down the main street that passed in front of the Buick facility, honking loudly, and displaying colorful signs.]

Although there are three lawyers in the Club, we all agree that legal activity should reinforce mass activity, not the other way around. A local bakery became notorious for its many discharges. Club members were involved in picketing, NLRB charges, and a lawsuit, and the number of discharges decreased dramatically. Executives of one of the very few businesses to move to Youngstown since the steel mills closed, Avanti Motors, told the media that if a union were organized they might leave town. The

Workers' Solidarity Club filed a charge with the NLRB. Avanti Motors was obliged to post a notice promising not to threaten a shutdown, and the UAW proceeded to organize at the plant.

OUR OWN UNION ORGANIZING

In evaluating the Trumbull strike, many Club members felt that our role had been essentially reactive. Union leaders made decisions about strategy. Rank-and-file union members and strike supporters had to live with these decisions whether or not they agreed with them. The sentiment was expressed that the Club should seek ways to do its own organizing.

This was a long process. Club members were involved in three attempts to organize unions. One was successful. A small group of visiting nurses and home health aides formed an independent union for which they (not we!) chose the name Visiting Nurses Solidarity. Two other organizing drives, at medium-size metal fabricators, failed.

STARTING YOUR OWN CLUB

There are a couple of things we would like to share with others who might want to try something similar.

First, from the very first meeting a majority of those present were rank-and-file workers, or retirees. Rather than fast-speaking professionals or academics setting the tone, it was the other way around. While lawyers and academics (including the director of labor studies at the local university) took part, they were minority voices.

Second, we discouraged lecturing, and rarely made long written presentations. We think that a broader consciousness grew naturally from the experience of talking and acting together. Having lived through the way big corporations trampled on people's lives in Youngstown, we found it easy to relate to Native Americans in the Southwest, or to Nicaragua. In 1988 four members of the Club went to Nicaragua and worked there for two weeks. One of them, an electric lineman, returned with a fellow worker to help bring electric power to small towns in northern Nicaragua.

Third, we didn't feel the need to come to a group decision about the correctness of a proposed action before a member did something. Instead the member said, "I'm planning to do so-and-so. I need help. Anyone who wants to give me a hand, meet me" at such-and-such a time and place. Acting in this way gave us a chance to try things out in practice. It was like the experimental method in science. We were able to draw conclusions from what worked and what didn't.[2]

---

2. This account appeared in *Labor Notes* 121 (April 1989), under the title "How We Built the Youngstown Workers' Solidarity Club." Several members of the Club helped to write it. Here and elsewhere in this edition, verb tenses have been changed to reflect the fact that this edition of *Solidarity Unionism* will appear almost a quarter century after many of the events described.

Solidarity USA

During and after World War II, management and organized labor in the United States undertook to provide through collective bargaining the "fringe benefits" that in other industrialized nations are financed by taxes and provided through the government. The pattern in communities like Youngstown was for people to work all their lives in one plant so as to become entitled to the pensions and medical insurance that such long service made possible. Workers took less in benefits because of the promise of benefits at retirement. They viewed pensions and medical insurance as deferred compensation, which they had fully earned by their labor at the time they retired.

This is the bargain that has collapsed under pressure from overseas competition. Corporations cannot now fulfill their promises to unions with respect to both pensions and medical benefits. A shrinking workforce in industries like steel cannot generate the cash flow needed to pay for the benefits of a much larger number of retirees.

The fringe benefit crisis came home to the Youngstown area when LTV Steel declared bankruptcy in July 1986. At the same time that it filed its bankruptcy petition, LTV Steel, a self-insured employer, directed the insurance companies that administered its benefit programs to stop paying medical and life insurance claims to retirees, about eleven thousand of them in or near Youngstown. The results were catastrophic. One retiree, Roy St. Clair, did not seek hospitalization for a heart attack because he did not know how he could pay the bill. He died a few hours later. Another retiree, Louis Lipka, blew his brains out in his bedroom because, according to his wife, he was worried about the family's benefits.

Delores Hrycyk, wife of a retiree with thirty-six years at Republic Steel (one of the companies merged to form LTV Steel), telephoned radio talk shows and called a rally in downtown Youngstown. A thousand people attended. Soon after they formed an organization with the name Solidarity USA. Between August 1986 and March 1987 the group took busloads of retirees to the bankruptcy court in New York City, to Washington, DC, to sympathetic city councils in Pittsburgh and Cleveland, and to Aliquippa, Pa., where on several occasions retirees sat down in the street leading to the mill gate. Thanks to such efforts medical insurance was restored, and as of September 1990, when LTV Steel came out of bankruptcy, LTV Steel retirees again received about the same pension and medical benefits they were receiving when LTV Steel declared bankruptcy.

A second generation of Solidarity USA leaders was elected in 1988. A newsletter was begun. The group met once a month at the Odd Fellows hall in Hubbard, Ohio, northeast of Youngstown.

The retirees who made up Solidarity USA had up to forty-odd years' seniority in Mahoning Valley steel mills. They prided themselves on keeping their contractual promises. Even in the 116-day strike of 1959, they recall, they found ways with the help of extended family members to make their mortgage payments and maintain their credit ratings. Now, they said, it was the company's turn to carry out contracts. Their slogan, chanted in innumerable Solidarity USA demonstrations, was: "We worked for it, we earned it, we want every penny of it."

The retirees had a complex relationship to the United Steelworkers of America. These men and women, in their fifties, sixties, and seventies, built the CIO in the Mahoning Valley. Many were local union officers and grievance committeemen. "Don't get me wrong," they will say. "I'm not anti-union. We built the union. We are the union!"

But these Youngstown retirees are bitterly disappointed in the union's representation, or lack thereof. They still speak about how they learned what was in the 1987 contract with LTV Steel at a meeting called by the Steelworkers in a local auditorium, at which active workers (who could vote on the contract) were seated in front, and retirees (who could not vote) were seated behind a rope at the rear. For its part, the union's International Executive Board described Solidarity USA as a "rump," made up of "dissidents" and possibly paid by the company.

Members of Solidarity USA were reluctant to spend their golden years in unending conflict with both company and union to preserve or restore promised benefits. In 1989, Solidarity USA endorsed national health insurance on the Canadian model. The discussion was interesting. A retiree group in Aliquippa proposed the creation of a Health Benefits Guaranty Corporation, similar to the Pension Benefit Guaranty Corporation. Solidarity USA was sympathetic but troubled. The problem with the Aliquippa project was that, if successful, it would ensure medical insurance only for those who had already won it through collective bargaining. Thirty to forty million citizens who had never had medical insurance would not be helped by the concept of guaranteeing benefits already bargained-for. In the end, Solidarity USA rousingly endorsed what I was careful to describe as "national health insurance," but the members called "socialized medicine."

Although at first made up almost entirely of retirees from LTV Steel, Solidarity USA attracted members from several other mills and fabricators, and for a time became a central labor body for retirees of all descriptions. The retirees who made up Solidarity USA, lacking any voice in the union, had no alternative to direct action. They marched on each other's picket lines in struggles with particular companies, and joined together to demand national health insurance.

It is a commentary on the state of the labor movement that nowhere have I seen such vitality as among retirees. They are not forced to belong to their organizations, hence they come to meetings gladly. Each retiree group makes its own decisions.

Meetings have both a social and an economic character. Participants sustain each other through the trials of growing old, as well as confronting together the latest modification in benefits they had supposed to be secure.

WORKERS AGAINST TOXIC CHEMICAL HAZARDS (WATCH)

WATCH was formed in 1988. The core of the group was four chemically poisoned workers from GM Lordstown, two White and two Black. Like retirees, they are no longer members of the union, and can only make themselves heard by direct action.

Their first step was to go through the obituaries in newspapers from Youngstown and nearby Warren for a period of eighteen months. Every time the paper reported the death of a former employee from GM Lordstown, they photocopied the obituary. Although the obituaries only occasionally provided the cause of death, they almost always indicated the person's age at time of death. WATCH members prepared a four by eight foot plywood board, painted white, with the names and ages at time of death of seventy-five persons who used to work at Lordstown hand-lettered in black. They called it the Lordstown Memorial (similar to the Vietnam Memorial in Washington, DC).

A press conference was planned to make public the Lordstown Memorial. Up to that time the union had stonewalled in response to WATCH complaints about conditions in the paint booths, and about the way fumes were emitted by one set of pipes and sucked back into the plant through another. The company, when it first saw a leaflet describing the Memorial, made a statement that WATCH members were malicious and their complaints were baseless. The press conference generated great publicity. Within a few weeks the union and company had decided to make a Proportional Mortality Ratio (PMR) study, comparing the number of deaths from cancer in the general population with the number of deaths from cancer among former Lordstown workers.

The study was released in September 1989. It showed that among former workers from the van and car assembly plants, the cancer death rate was a third higher than in the general population. Among former workers in the fab plant, where toxic coolants and lubricants are used in cutting metal, the cancer death rate was a half higher than normal.

On Workers' Memorial Day in April 1990, WATCH held a citizens' hearing on toxic chemicals, at which workers from many plants in the Valley testified about the substances they use and the problems those substances cause.

Summary

I don't want to claim too much for the self-activity of these groups in the Mahoning Valley. Two of the three groups (the Workers' Solidarity Club and WATCH) were very small. Solidarity USA, which grew to be much larger, came into being when a major employer went bankrupt and gradually diminished when the company came out of bankruptcy with benefits more or less fully restored.

However, these entities seem to show that the labor organizations we have now are not inevitable: that there are alternatives. The Workers' Solidarity Club, Solidarity USA and WATCH suggest that a qualitatively different kind of labor organization *is* possible right now.

Groups like the Workers' Solidarity Club, Solidarity USA and WATCH differ from existing trade unions in the following ways:

- Membership in an existing union is compulsory, once it is recognized by the employer or certified by the National Labor Relations Board as exclusive bargaining representative.[3] In contrast, membership in the Workers' Solidarity Club, Solidarity USA, and WATCH, was voluntary.

- Dues are deducted by the employer from the pay checks of members of existing unions. The Workers' Solidarity Club and Solidarity USA raised substantial sums of money by passing the hat.

- Existing unions are led by paid, full-time officers and staff personnel, except in the smaller local unions. None of the three Youngstown organizations had paid officers or staff.

- In existing unions, the desire of local union officers and others to be promoted to full-time staff jobs creates an atmosphere of conformity and servile deference. An example is the insipid union press, which reports only victories and in which critical and independent voices are almost never heard. On the other hand, in the Workers' Solidarity Club, Solidarity USA and WATCH, discussion was freewheeling and no one was safe from criticism.

----

3. In "right to work" states, state law prohibits collective bargaining agreements that require all workers in a unionized shop to belong to a union. I oppose "right to work" laws; but I think solidarity unions should voluntarily *choose* not to require union membership. Professor Charles Morris has argued that the National Labor Relations Act requires employers to bargain with so-called "minority" or "members only" unions on behalf of the members of such unions, even though the union includes only a minority of workers at a particular workplace.

- The activity of existing unions is legalistic. Collective bargaining agreements are thick and hard to read. The answer to all problems that arise on the shop floor is, "file a grievance." The three Mahoning Valley groups, on the contrary, succeeded by a variety of imaginative direct actions.

In the remainder of this book, I propose to explore whether groups like the Workers' Solidarity Club, Solidarity USA, and WATCH represent a practical alternative to existing unions.

I want to suggest, as an hypothesis to be tested in the course of our common work, that the time has come to break with the forms of organization of the existing labor movement. This doesn't necessarily mean working outside existing unions. It means that whether we work within or outside existing structures, we must self-consciously seek the emergence of new forms. I want to suggest that trade unions as they exist in the United States are structurally incapable of changing the corporate economy, so that simply electing new officers to head these organizations will not solve our problems. I argue that the internationalization of capital, far from proving that such centralized unions are needed more than ever, has, on the contrary, demonstrated their impotence and the need for something qualitatively new.

In the next part of the book we will take a look at the origins of CIO business unionism. I am going to show that in the early 1930s there were rank-and-file committees, independent local unions, and networks of local action groups, that were a lot like the Workers' Solidarity Club, Solidarity USA, and WATCH. I will also propose that the big CIO unions were from the beginning a very different kind of organization, organized from the top down, dependent on government support, committed to regulating shopfloor action through collective bargaining, hostile to independent labor politics.

Then we'll talk about the historical roots of alternative kinds of organization, like the shopfloor committee and the parallel central labor union, and ask: In addition to being congenial, can such organizational forms be effective?

And finally, I will comment briefly on the spirit of solidarity in which we try to build these new forms.

Chapter Two

DISPOSE
OF OLD
OR USED
WORKERS
HERE

KONOPACKI

What Happened in the 1930s

RANK-AND-FILE STRUGGLES IN THE EARLY 1930S

MANY PEOPLE—NOT ONLY WORKERS BUT ALSO HISTORIANS and labor lawyers—think that the modern labor movement in the United States began in the mid-1930s when John L. Lewis founded the CIO. They date the beginning of the movement from 1935, when Lewis socked Bill Hutcheson at the AFL national convention, and together with other leaders started the Committee for Industrial Organization, or from 1936, when these leaders took their unions out of the AFL and changed the name of their network to the Congress of Industrial Organizations.

But this was the second or third chapter in a story that began earlier, around 1932. Union bureaucrats like Lewis, of the United Mine Workers, and Sidney Hillman, president of the Amalgamated Clothing Workers, seized an opportunity that resulted from a phenomenal upsurge of self-organization by rank-and-file workers in the years 1933–1935.[1]

---

1. See *"We Are All Leaders": The Alternative Unionism of the Early 1930s*, ed. Staughton Lynd (Urbana: University of Illinois Press, 1996).

The rank-and-file struggles of the early 1930s, before the passage of the National Labor Relations Act (or Wagner Act), and before the founding of the CIO, had certain common features. They were generally organized from below, by committees of ordinary workers who teamed up with others in their shops and with other workers in the community where they all lived. And they relied on direct action, above all on the strike.

I tried to piece together the story in the steel industry at a time when many of those who took part were still alive.[2] In June 1933, the feeble AFL union in the steel industry reported less than five thousand members. A year later, in April 1934, the membership was somewhere between fifty thousand and two hundred thousand. Harvey O'Connor, then a labor reporter living in Pittsburgh, remembered it this way:

Along came the New Deal, and then came the NRA [National Recovery Act], and the effect was electric all up and down those valleys. The mills began reopening somewhat, and the steelworkers read in the newspapers about this NRA Section 7A that guaranteed you the right to organize. All over the steel country union locals sprang up spontaneously. Not by virtue of the Amalgamated Association [the AFL union in steel]; they couldn't have cared less. But these locals sprang up at Duquesne,

---

2. Staughton Lynd, "The Possibility of Radicalism in the Early 1930s: The Case of Steel," in *Workers' Struggles, Past and Present: A "Radical America" Reader*, ed. James Green (Philadelphia: Temple University Press, 1983), pp.190–208.

Homestead, and Braddock. You name the mill town and there was a local there, carrying a name like the "Blue Eagle" or the "New Deal" local. These people had never had any experience in unionism. All they knew was that, by golly, the time had come when they could organize and the Government guaranteed them the right to organize!

This tremendous increase in union membership was brought about by workers themselves, not by full-time union organizers. At U.S. Steel's Edgar Thomson works in Braddock, for example, an Amalgamated organizer provided membership cards and volunteer organizers from the mill returned in a week with five hundred of them signed. From 1933 to 1934 steelworkers themselves signed up about the same number of workers that the CIO, using two hundred full-time organizers, later signed up in a comparable period of time, from June 1936 to March 1937.

A similar process took place on West Coast docks among longshoremen, seamen, and other waterfront workers. Workers organized through a small waterfront bulletin called the *Waterfront Worker*, which first appeared in December 1932, and a rank-and-file caucus that met in a hall on Albion Street in San Francisco, and was often referred to as the Albion Hall group. Both the paper and the caucus called for an active, militant union presence on the job, through committees at each workplace, with representation on the union's governing boards.[3]

---

3. Bruce Nelson, *Workers on the Waterfront: Seamen, Longshoremen,*

Much remains to be done, and needs to be done while human and documentary sources are still available, to uncover the history of these years—in other places and industries. Consider Barberton, Ohio, a town west of Akron that in the 1930s had less than twenty-five thousand residents. In Barberton, workers in rubber, match, chemical, and insulator factories joined in December 1933 to create the Barberton Central Labor Union. There being as yet no CIO, they created independent "federal" unions directly linked to the national AFL without belonging to any national union for that particular industry. Joining a union in Barberton, writes researcher John Borsos, was similar to joining a church. When one group of workers went on strike, other workers in that small city united to support the strike as a matter of community solidarity.

The words of one activist quoted by Borsos expressed a pervasive Barberton union attitude: "When the B&W was on strike, we were all on strike. The PPG, the Ohio Brass, it didn't matter. We were like a family."[4]

Historians have debated whether these workers who supported each others' strikes and, on occasion, occupied their factories, wanted anything more than union recognition and collective bargaining. At a minimum, it seems clear, they also wanted increased control over their immediate

and Unionism in the 1930s (Urbana: University of Illinois Press, 1988), chapter 4.

4. John Borsos, "'We Make You This Appeal in the Name of Every Working Man and Woman in Barberton': Solidarity Unionism in Barberton, Ohio, 1933–1941," in *"We Are All Leaders,"* pp. 238–93.

work conditions. Even after the passage of the Wagner Act and the formation of the CIO, the first victories for industrial unionism came from below, through extralegal rank-and-file sitdown strikes at the Akron rubber plants and the General Motors plants in Flint, Michigan. In rubber and auto plants, on the San Francisco waterfront, in "Little Steel" mills like the Inland Steel mill near Chicago, workers used their new unions to assert control over their work through wildcat strikes, slowdowns and other kinds of direct action.

GOVERNMENT SPONSORSHIP OF THE CIO

CIO unions came into being in the context of the National Labor Relations Act as exclusive collective bargaining agents certified by the state. Prior to the 1930s, labor organizations in the United States—whatever their other differences—had jealously guarded the concept of union independence and autonomy. In contrast, the desired objective of CIO unions was to become legal monopolies, complete with enforced membership (union shop) and a source of income independent of any continuing accountability of unions to their members (dues check-off).

The danger of such state sponsorship for an independent, radical labor movement was clearly perceived at the time. The Industrial Workers of the World (IWW), the Communist Party prior to the Seventh Congress of the Comintern in 1935, the American Civil Liberties Union, and independent radicals like A.J. Muste, for this reason opposed—or expressed grave reservations about—passage of the National Labor Relations Act.

In 1934, when the first version of the Act was proposed, Mary Van Kleeck of the ACLU wrote to the Act's principal sponsor, Senator Robert Wagner, advising him that the ACLU would oppose his bill because of the "inevitable trends of its administration." Van Kleeck explained that

> The danger is that the effort to regulate industrial relations by requiring of employers certain "fair practices," while appearing to impose those obligations upon them, necessarily brings the whole subject within the scope of government regulation. This involves a certain assumption as to a status quo. To prevent or discourage strikes which have for their purpose gradual increase in the workers' power in a period when fundamental economic change in the ownership of industry can clearly be envisaged may only serve to check the rising power of the exponents of human rights, and indeed to protect private property rights in exchange for obligations which are likely to be merely the least common denominator of industrial practice.

Van Kleeck concluded by acknowledging that Senator Wagner's bill explicitly protected the right of workers to strike, but "insisted that pressures would inevitably be exerted on the National Labor Relations Board to discourage strikes in favor of less disruptive methods of resolving conflicts." About the same time ACLU president Roger Baldwin, writing to Senator David Walsh, agreed that the machinery proposed by the pending legislation would "impair labor's rights in the long run, however much its authors may intend precisely the contrary."[5]

In 1935, this time in response to the final version of the Wagner Act, Baldwin wrote to Wagner that the ACLU would oppose the creation of a National Labor Relations Board "on the ground that no such federal agency intervening in the conflicts between employers and employees can be expected fairly to determine the issues of labor's rights. We say this from a long experience with the various boards set up in Washington, all of which have tended to conciliation, or, in some cases, arbitration." Baldwin urged Wagner to consider "the view that the pressures on any government agency from employers are so constant and determined that it is far better to have no governmental intervention than to suffer the delusion that it will aid labor in its struggle for the rights to organize, bargain collectively and strike."

---

5. Senator Wagner's aide and principal draftsperson of the National Labor Relations Act, Leon Keyserling, shared this apprehension. He told an interviewer that Section 13 of the Act sought to protect the right to strike in the most explicit terms "because Wagner was always strong for the right to strike on the ground that without the right to strike, which was labor's ultimate weapon, they really had no other weapon. That guarantee was a part of his thinking. It was particularly necessary because a lot of people made the argument that because the government was giving labor the right to bargain collectively, that was a substitute for the right to strike, which was utterly wrong." Kenneth M. Casebeer, "Holder of the Pen: An Interview with Leon Keyserling on Drafting the Wagner Act," *University of Miami Law Review* 42, no. 3 (November 1987), p. 353.

Even before the Wagner Act had been passed and the CIO had been founded, these critics accurately forecast the domestication and decline of a labor movement sponsored by the government.

CIO CONTRACTUALISM

CIO unions were from the outset committed to contractualism, that is, to the regulation of relations between employer and employee by means of a legally binding collective bargaining agreement that (a) forbids strikes for the duration of the contract, and (b) cedes management decisions to the employer. The very first contracts between General Motors and the UAW, and between United States Steel and the Steel Workers Organizing Committee, in the spring of 1937, contained clauses prohibiting strikes for the duration of the contract. There was never a time when the leaders of CIO unions opposed such language. Indeed, they presented themselves to management as guarantors of labor peace.

Similarly, the "management prerogatives clause" typical in CIO contracts today was part of the very first collective bargaining agreement with U.S. Steel in 1937. Then the clause stated: "The management of the works and the direction of the working forces, including the right to hire, suspend or discharge for proper cause, or transfer, and the right to relieve employees from duty because of lack of work or for other legitimate reasons, is vested exclusively in the Corporation."

Essentially the same words appear in the present U.S. Steel contract: "The Company retains the exclusive rights to manage the business and plants and to direct the working forces. . . . The rights to manage the business and plants and to direct the working forces include the rights to hire, suspend or discharge for proper cause, or transfer, and the right to relieve employees from duty because of lack of work or for other legitimate reason."

There was an intimate connection between government sponsorship of CIO organization, and the fact that CIO unions from the beginning negotiated contracts containing no-strike and management prerogative clauses. The preamble to the Wagner Act identified its principal object as labor peace. CIO leaders acted the part they knew to be expected from them if they were to receive ongoing support from the government. Radical labor journalist Len DeCaux wrote in April 1935 that when Lewis and other union officials testified before the Senate committee considering the Wagner Act, the labor leaders said in effect: "Allow the workers to organize, establish strong governmental machinery for dealing with labor questions, and industrial peace will result."

CIO Hostility to Independent Labor Politics

The rank-and-file workers who advocated industrial unionism in the early 1930s also advocated independent labor politics. Between the years 1932 and 1936 local labor parties fielded candidates in Cambridge, New Bedford, and Springfield, Massachusetts; Berlin and Lincoln, New Hampshire;

Danbury and Hartford, Connecticut; Buffalo and New York City; Allentown and Philadelphia, Pennsylvania; Akron, Canton, and Toledo, Ohio; Detroit, Hamtramck, and Port Huron, Michigan; Chicago and Hillsboro, Illinois; Sioux Falls, South Dakota; Everett and Goldbar, Washington; and San Francisco, California. In at least ten other communities central labor unions endorsed the idea of a labor party, as did the State Federations of Labor of Rhode Island, Vermont, New Jersey, and Wisconsin. And at the 1935 AFL convention, a resolution endorsing a labor party lost by only 108 votes to 104.

The leaders of CIO unions from the very beginning opposed all steps toward independent political action. Sidney Hillman persuaded the Amalgamated to renounce its traditional commitment to a labor party and to endorse Roosevelt in 1936. At the UAW convention that same year, delegates first voted unanimously for a resolution calling for the formation of a national labor party, and defeated a resolution to back FDR. Only when Lewis made a personal plea to the convention and Adolf Germer, one of his lieutenants, issued a private warning to UAW president Homer Martin, did the delegates reverse themselves. Overall, the organization of Labor's Nonpartisan League in April 1936 by Lewis, Hillman, and their associates, bankrolled by half a million dollars from the UMW alone and single-mindedly devoted to reelecting Roosevelt, was the kiss of death for independent labor politics for years to come.

This was not the necessary consequence of voting for Franklin Roosevelt in national elections. Berlin, New Hampshire overwhelmingly supported FDR at the same time that it voted into power a local labor party. CIO activists could have supported Roosevelt's candidacies while putting their main energies into building local political movements independent of the Democratic Party. As late as 1946, the sociologist C. Wright Mills found that a third of local CIO officials favored immediate formation of a labor party. But national CIO leaders—less than 10 percent of whom shared this sentiment—said no.[6]

SUMMARY

There is a temptation to romanticize the early history of the CIO and to say to each other: If only we could go back to the way the CIO was in 1936, or 1945.

The truth is that from the very beginning CIO unions set out to control and suppress the insurgent, rank-and-file groupings that had tried to organize industrial unions and to form independent labor parties in the early 1930s. From the very beginning, CIO unions:

- first, were government-sponsored monopolies that tried to force all persons working in a particular shop to join the union, and sought to deduct dues from the worker's paycheck;

---

6. The successful election of a local labor party in Berlin, New Hampshire, is narrated by Eric Leif Davin and Staughton Lynd, "Picket Line and Ballot Box: The Forgotten Legacy of the Local Labor Party Movement, 1932–1936," *Radical History Review* 22 (Winter 1979–80), pp. 42–63.

- second, agreed to collective bargaining agreements containing, on the one hand, a management
  prerogatives clause that enabled management
  unilaterally to make the crucial investment decisions about whether a plant would stay open, how
  profits were to be invested, and so on, and, on the
  other hand, a no-strike clause prohibiting direct
  action of all forms during the life of the contract;
- third, sought to undermine and prevent the formation of independent labor parties, locally and
  nationally.

Chapter Three

Is There an Alternative to the Unionism We Have Now?

THERE IS NO WAY TO PROVE IN ADVANCE THAT THERE IS A realistic alternative to CIO business unionism. We can only prove that an alternative is possible by doing it, making it happen.

Still, there are some useful things that we can say to each other at this point in time, to help us make the attempt. In this section of the book I will, first, try to pinpoint the essential difference in principle between the existing unionism and the unionism some of us are trying to build, and then, show that at various times in the past shopfloor committees and parallel central labor unions like those we are beginning to build have been very effective indeed. After that I will ask brothers and sisters reading these pages not to be afraid of the word "socialism." Socialism is the only practical alternative to capitalism. We should turn our attention to defining clearly what kind of socialism we want.

SOLIDARITY UNIONISM

The essential principle of CIO business unions is verticalism. They are hierarchical organizations. Power flows from the top down: the international union officers appoint the staff men, the district directors depend on the international union for their share of the dues check-off money, the staff men take over the local union grievances after the first couple of steps, the grievance committeemen settle grievances without consulting the men who filed the grievances and who, more than anyone, are affected by how the grievances are settled.

If you like things done this way, you can stop reading right here. You may want to put your energy into electing new officers to run these top-down unions.

But if you don't like things done this way, a moment's thought will lead to the conclusion that the structure of hierarchical unions will not change simply by electing new people to run them. You will start looking for alternative kinds of structure.

The essential principle of the alternative kind of structure that one glimpses in the 1930s, or in the very small steps that workers in Youngstown made in the 1980s and 1990s, is solidarity. Alternative unionism is solidarity unionism. It is relying, not on technical expertise, or on numbers of signed-up members, nor yet on bureaucratic chain-of-command, but on the spark that leaps from person to person, especially in times of common crisis.

A college teacher or a lawyer is likely to experience victory or defeat as a personal matter. Victories are felt to be personal coups. If a big case is lost, or one fails to get tenure, it is believed to be due to some personal act or omission. Similarly, the wins and losses of others are perceived as these others' private business.

Most workers, on the other hand, are forced to recognize that the power of the employer is much greater than that of any single employee, acting alone. The Horatio Alger myth that individual punctuality and application can overcome all obstacles does not correspond with the powerlessness experienced in a mine disaster, or a plant shutdown. It follows that the only realistic way to try to deal with such common problems is to act together.

The words, "an injury to one is an injury to all," express this understanding. Above all, this understanding is expressed in the action of ordinary rank-and-file workers, when they walk off the job in support of each other, or in other ways take risks for the good of all.

Consider the beginning of Polish Solidarity.

When Anna Walentynowicz was fired from her job as a crane operator in the Lenin shipyard in Gdansk, Poland, in August 1980, her workmates struck demanding her reinstatement. Other shipyards struck in sympathy. In two days the workers at the Lenin yard had won their demands. Walentynowicz and Lech Walesa were reinstated, and the Polish government promised to build a monument honoring workers killed in the strike of 1970.

The question was posed whether the Lenin yard strikers should stay out on behalf of the demands of other shipyards. As Walentynowicz tells the story:[1]

---

1. "The Woman Behind Solidarity: The Story of Anna Walentynowicz," *Ms.*, February 1984, p. 96. (See also the obituary for Alina Pienkowska, *New York Times*, October 28, 2002, which also credits Ms. Pienkowska for the decisive action on August 16, 1980, that caused the strike at the Lenin yard to be continued.)

Alina Pienkowska and I went running back to the hall
to declare a solidarity strike, but the microphones were
off. The shipyard loudspeakers were announcing that the
strike was over and that everyone had to leave by six P.M.
The gates were open, and people were leaving.

So Alina and I went running to the main gate. And
I began to appeal to them to declare a solidarity strike,
because the only reason that the manager had met our demands was that the other factories were still on strike. I said
that if the workers at these other factories were defeated, we
wouldn't be safe either. But somebody challenged me. "On
whose authority are you declaring this a strike? I'm tired and
I want to go home." I too was tired, and I started to cry. . . .

Now, Alina is very small. A tiny person, but full of
initiative. She stood up on a barrel and began to appeal
to those who were leaving. "We have to help the others
with their strikes, because they have helped us. We have
to defend them." Somebody from the crowd said, "She's
right!" The gate was closed.

The strike that gave birth to Polish Solidarity followed.
At the moment of crisis, Walentynowicz and Pienkowska
took the position that only if the Lenin workers continued
their strike on behalf of the workers at the other shipyards
would the Lenin workers be "safe." Clearly she was saying
that workers, to preserve their rights, need above all else to
preserve their solidarity.

Another example of solidarity comes from Guatemala.
In February 1984, the owners of its Coca Cola plant

announced that the enterprise was a failure, and closed the plant. According to historian Jack Spence: "The workers immediately occupied the premises. The owners then offered about 6 months severance pay. The workers demanded that the money be used to keep the plant in operation."[2] The owners soon thereafter left the country. The workers addressed their demands to Coca-Cola International. "As days stretched into payless weeks, and weeks into months, about one hundred workers had to drop out. Of the remainder, eighty were organized into work teams to support the families of all. The rest divided into two work teams, each occupying the factory for 24 hour shifts." It took more than a year to find a new owner, and to reopen the plant. But the new owner agreed to hire only 265 of the workers putting the remainder on a first-hire waiting list, with no requirement that any of them be hired. Professor Spence inquired if the 85 who did not go back to work were the workers with least seniority. No, he was told, "eighty-five volunteers stepped forward to place themselves on the waiting list. They had been out of work for almost a year."

A last example of solidarity, showing that North American workers can do it just as well as any one else, is the inspiring story of clerical and technical workers at Yale

---

2. Jack Spence, "Guatemala: 1985," *Resist Newsletter*, No. 179 (October 1985). In layoff situations workers have often decided not to follow seniority but to divide the available work equally. See *"We Are All Leaders,"* p. 3, and Mia Giunta, "Sharing the Work," in *Rank and File* (Chicago: Haymarket Books, 2011), pp. 322–34.

University.[3] In organizing a union, in negotiating a first contract, Local 34 and its organizers wrote a textbook on solidarity unionism. The union rejected the use of literature for the first year of its drive, and made no efforts to get members to sign union cards for over a year and a half. Instead its organizers, mostly rank-and-file workers, endlessly talked with individuals and small groups.

> When one of the organizers first approached Beverly Lott, "He didn't say, 'Just sign a card'." What he said was, "I want you to do some work. I want you to help, because it's going to be your union, not my union, because I'm going to be gone some day."

All committees were open to any member; the Organizing Committee came to have 450 members. Not only did Local 34 pledge not to collect any initiation fees or dues until a first contract had been secured, it also promised that the members would set their own dues.

The most dramatic expression of solidarity at Yale came from the blue-collar service and maintenance workers in Local 35. They had been organized for years, and clerical workers had regularly crossed their picket lines. Yet when the clerical workers struck for a contract, the members of Local 35 stayed out.

---

3. Toni Gilpin, Gary Isaac, Dan Letwin, and Jack McKivigan, *On Strike for Respect: The Yale Strike of 1984–1985* (Chicago: Charles H. Kerr Publishing Company, 1988).

> [T]he administration sent a personal letter to each member of Local 35 threatening disciplinary action against those who failed to come to work. . . . On the evening of October 2, five hundred members of Local 35 assembled at the Methodist Church and marched to President Giamatti's house, where each deposited in a box . . . a small blue card reading, "I'm out. I have a right to be out. I'm staying out. Yale should settle or arbitrate."

SHOPFLOOR COMMITTEES

When I speak of a shopfloor or stewards' committee, I mean a committee based in the informal work groups that Stan Weir writes about, made up of elected representatives who continue to work full-time.

Informal work groups, as Stan Weir has described them, come to provide for their members what amounts to a family-on-the-job. "Led by natural on-the-job leaders, they conduct daily guerrilla skirmishes with their employers and often against their official union representatives. These groups are the power base for insurgencies from below." In Youngstown, I have repeatedly dealt with shops where workers felt unserved or abandoned by union leaders, and elected a committee to represent them better. The persons elected to such committees tend to be individuals who have earned the trust of their fellow workers on the shop floor over a period of years.

I also mean a committee that may exist in a non-union shop, or, where a union has been recognized, may function alongside the official union structure. It is an idea that goes far back in our country's labor history.

David Montgomery, for example, has described how in the era of World War I workers formed elected committees in individual plants to stand up to the employer through direct action. Thus at the Westinghouse plant near Pittsburgh, workers created an "in-plant organization made up of their own elected delegates" that cut across traditional craft lines. The permanent presence of this active group representative right there on the shop floor, "all day every day," added something essential to the very different kind of representation that a national union could offer. At Westinghouse, as Montgomery tells the story, workers recruited employees of all descriptions (including clerical workers) into an organization marvelously named the Allegheny Congenial Industrial Union. This organization "copied the IWW by devoting itself to struggles around demands, rather than negotiating contracts, . . . but it also used a system of departmental delegates inside the plant as its basic structure."[4]

The improvised shop committee at Westinghouse in the World War I period may be compared to the shopfloor activities carried on in industries such as steel, auto, rubber, and electrical equipment during the early days of the CIO at a time when unions were not yet exclusive bargaining agents, collective bargaining agreements had not been signed, and, as a result, shop stewards were still free to orchestrate

---

4. David Montgomery, *The Fall of the House of Labor: The Workplace, the State and American Labor Activism, 1865–1925* (Cambridge: Cambridge University Press, 1987), pp. 317–19.

slowdowns and wildcat strikes in support of their constituents' demands.

John Sargent, first president of the CIO union at Inland Steel in East Chicago, Indiana, tells what happened there in the years between the Little Steel Strike of 1937 and the beginning of World War II in 1941.

> Without a contract, without any agreement with the company, without any regulations concerning hours of work, conditions of work, or wages, a tremendous surge took place. We talk of a rank-and-file movement, the beginning of union organization was the best kind of rank-and-file movement you could think of. John L. Lewis sent in a few organizers, but there were no organizers at Inland Steel, and I'm sure there were no organizers at Youngstown Sheet and Tube. The union organizers were essentially workers in the mill who were so disgusted with their conditions and so ready for a change that they took the union into their own hands.
>
> For example, what happened at Inland Steel I believe is perhaps representative of what happened throughout the steel industry. Without a contract we secured for ourselves agreements on working conditions and wages that we do not have today, and that were better by far than what we do have today in the mill. For example as a result of the enthusiasm of the people in the mill you had a series of strikes, wildcats, shut-downs, slow-downs, anything working people could think of to secure for themselves what they decided they had to have. If

wages were low there was no contract to prohibit them from striking, and they struck for better wages. If their conditions were bad, if they didn't like what was going on, if they were being abused, the people in the mills themselves— without a contract or any agreement with the company involved—would shut down a department or even a group of departments to secure for themselves the things they found necessary.

We had an agreement with Inland Steel way back in '38 or '39 that the company would not pay less than any of its competitors throughout the country. We never had it so good, I assure you of that. All you had to do as a union representative was come into the company and say, "Look, we have a group of people working in the pickle line, and at Youngstown, Ohio or Youngstown Sheet and Tube in East Chicago people are getting more money than we're getting for the same job." And if that was a fact, we were given an increase in wages at Inland. In those departments where you had a strong group of union members, where they were most active, we had the highest rates in the country. We were never able to secure conditions of this kind after we secured contracts.[5]

The same thing happened during the late 1930s in automobile plants. At the GM plant in Atlanta, one participant recalls:

---

5. John Sargent, "Your Dog Don't Bark No More," in *Rank and File* (Chicago: Haymarket Books, 2011), pp. 107–8.

Now actually in the signed agreement we didn't get anything except recognition for our members only. We were not permitted to bargain for anyone but our members. But, I think, following the settlement of the strike we had some of the most effective bargaining in the plant that I think we ever had, because of the way we handled it.

The company wanted to bargain with the people individually, so they adopted what they called an open-door policy. The manager's door was always open. Any employee could come in and discuss any problems he had with them at any time. And what we did, in the departments, one employee had a problem, we all had a problem, and we would all go down to the office to discuss our problem with them. Now that shut the whole plant down, because they had to settle the department's problem before they could get the plant to operate.

Such "solidarity unionism," inspired by and permeated with the spirit of solidarity, should be distinguished from a merely tactical use of solidarity.

For example, the AFL-CIO pamphlet, *The Inside Game*, although subtitled *Winning with Workplace Strategies*, presents a tactical rather than a strategic or principled argument for solidarity.

The booklet begins promisingly. In situations where a strike would be ineffective, it suggests, "staying on the job and working from the inside may be more appropriate and effective." What does this mean? *The Inside Game* explains:

Increasingly, unions are finding they must actually *go back in time* to find ways to cope with the refusal of employers to bargain in a fair and equitable manner.

Back to a time when there was no National Labor Relations Act, no public employee collective bargaining laws.

Back to a time when the only rule was that *there were no rules* and workers had only their numbers, their solidarity and their aggressive collective actions to protect their jobs and pry contracts from employers.

The Inside Game goes on to say that one of the names unions have given to these techniques is simply, "building solidarity."

Case studies at the end of *The Inside Game* include provocative specific ideas, such as:

1. When the contract runs out, go on working and ask members to pay union dues voluntarily;
2. "Work to rule" by refusing to work outside job descriptions or to work overtime;
3. Sit-downs in such large numbers that the employer will hesitate to fire or arrest all those involved;
4. Holding regular meetings on the shop floor as well as at the union hall;
5. Setting up a voluntary "Solidarity Fund" to assist fellow workers fired or disciplined;
6. Mass presentation of grievances, by workers who leave their work stations and go to management offices to complain;

7. Expanding the number of stewards to include more people holding key jobs in the plant;

8. Boycotting company Christmas parties, banquets and dinners;

9. Taking over in-plant meetings called by the company;

10. "[S]inging solidarity songs in the employee cafeteria just below the executive offices."

These are indeed the sorts of actions by means of which rank-and-file workers built CIO unions in the 1930s. But do the authors of *The Inside Game* intend that this "building solidarity" style of action become a way of life? Do they, for example, seek to institutionalize the abolition of the dues check-off, or direct action on the shop floor, or a shop steward for every foreman?

Not on your life! The object of solidarity tactics is said by *The Inside Game* to be convincing the employer "that a decent contract is in management's own self-interest": that is, by convincing the employer that conventional bargaining, in which the employer can deal with full-time representatives who in turn act as policemen of their own rank and file, is preferable to rank-and-file mass action.

This is exactly what John L. Lewis did fifty years ago, when the CIO was organized. He used the radical direct action of the sitdown at Flint, Michigan, in January–February 1937 to frighten Myron Taylor of U.S. Steel into recognizing the Steel Workers Organizing Committee in March 1937. Once the CIO unions had been recognized as responsible bargaining partners with whom management could negotiate "a decent contract . . . in management's own self-interest," Lewis got rid of the radicals who built the CIO.

The critical analytical error of *The Inside Game*, as in the general thinking of established unions about their current crisis, is the assumption that labor and management have the same or mutually consistent interests. The dominant organizations in the American labor movement for the past century have made this assumption. It is the assumption that underlies business unionism, because it induces trade unions to leave investment decisions to management while directing their own attention to wages, hours, and working conditions, and to surrender the right to strike (for the duration of collective bargaining agreements) in the belief that workers no longer need the strike to protect their day-to-day interests.

Parallel Central Labor Bodies

Equally deep-rooted in the labor history of the United States is another kind of committee, the council in which the local unions or rank-and-file groups from different places of work in a locality make contact with each other, broaden one another's consciousness, and take common action.

The official AFL-CIO central labor body purports to be such an entity, and there are situations in which it will actually function as such. In other circumstances, workers will have to organize new entities—parallel central labor bodies like the Workers' Solidarity Club of Youngstown—to perform this function.

David Montgomery describes how at the same Westinghouse plant described earlier, a key organizer was dismissed. Two thousand men and women walked out. By the next morning, thirteen thousand striking workers linked hands to form a huge human chain around the Westinghouse complex. Giant processions of strikers and supporters gradually closed down the whole Monongahela Valley. On November 1, 1916, a parade bedecked with red flags and led by a Lithuanian band, invaded steel mills, chain works, and machinery companies, bringing out thirty-six thousand workers. "The ethnic antagonisms that have absorbed the attention of most historians studying the region's workers seemed to melt away, as the angry and joyous tide of humanity poured through the streets."[6]

Essentially the same thing happened in the local general strikes in Minneapolis, Toledo, and San Francisco in 1934. And by whatever name—"district assemblies" in the era of the Knights of Labor, or IWW "mixed locals," or "soviets" in the Russian Revolutions of 1905 and 1917, or local branches of Polish Solidarity—the bodies that coordinate such actions rely not so much on the national organization of all workers in a given craft or industry as on the solidarity of all workers in a particular place.

Again the 1930s prove to be a storehouse of alternatives, as the Los Angeles Labor Networking Committee indicates in its position paper, "The Failure of Business Unionism and the Emergence of a Rank-and-File Alternative." The paper gives the following examples of "history to be retrieved."

---

6. Montgomery, *Fall of the House of Labor*, pp. 322–25.

Out of a sitdown strike in the Hormel plant at Austin, Minnesota, in 1933 emerged the Independent Union of All Workers (IUAW). It contained meatpacking workers, grocery clerks, butchers, waitresses, bartenders, and many more. All who were employed . . . could join. Like most rank-and-file organizing efforts at that time, the IUAW was deeply rooted in both workplaces and the general community. It made substantial headway in south-central Minnesota. . . . [T]he IUAW affiliated with the CIO as soon as the new federation came out of the AFL. Representatives of CIO President John L. Lewis immediately split the IUAW into several parts and redistributed them into different international union organizing committees. (How valuable an IUAW-type structure would have been to local P-9 forty-two years later when its 4,000 members were individually forced to take permanent wage cuts in order to loan Hormel the money to build an automated plant nearby which eliminated over 2,500 jobs.)

[Similarly,] the Maritime Federation of the Pacific (MFP) was formed out of the general Pacific Coast maritime strike of 1934 by separate unions of longshoremen, deckhands, ship's engine room workers, waiters, cooks and stewards, radio operators, mates and engineers. Each grouping had a specific union to concentrate on problems affecting their particular jobs, but all together could move against the employers as a single unit whenever necessary.

The MFP formalized this waterfront community alliance. In San Francisco the four largest participating unions—the International Longshoremen and Warehousemen; Sailors Union of the Pacific; Marine Firemen, Oilers, Watertenders and Wipers; and the Marine Cooks and Stewards—all had their hiring halls, offices and meeting halls in the Alaska Fishermen's Union Building, a half block off the Embarcadero, just north of Market Street. The always present antagonisms of the labor market were daily minimized by the friendships struck in the nearby bars and cafes.

The breakdown of the MFP and its parallel on the Gulf Coast occurred . . . because the rank-and-file approach did not conform to that of important AFL officials, including those who would soon form the CIO.

We are not speaking of some organizational chart that anyone will impose on the wonderful variety of workers' self-organization. The point is just the reverse: that these two kinds of committees—the committee formed at the individual workplace, with its elected delegates or stewards, and the committee of all kinds of workers in a given locality—recur and recur whenever working people organize for themselves, without somebody telling them what to do or how to do it.

A New Kind of Socialism

The social system that fell apart in the Eastern Europe and the Soviet Union, and was brutally preserved in China, is not socialism, but communism.

"Communism" is a word with two meanings. Marx used it in his *Critique of the Gotha Program* to mean a second or higher stage of post-capitalist society. In the first stage of post-capitalist society, which Marx called "socialism," people would still be paid on the basis of the work each had performed rather than on the basis of need. The slogan of such a socialist society, Marx wrote, would be: "to each according to his work." A communist society would come into being when the economy was so productive that distribution could be on the basis of need. The slogan of that society, according to Marx, would be: "from each according to his ability, to each according to his need."

Communism has come to have a second meaning, which is a society in which public ownership of the means of production is accompanied by political dictatorship. This is the communism that exists, or existed until 1989, from East Germany to North Korea as well as in Cuba.

This second use of the word "communism" to mean political dictatorship in a publicly owned economy also owes something to Marx. Marx believed that the transition from capitalist to post-capitalist society was unlikely to come about peacefully. He thought it would be necessary for the working class, once in possession of state power, to exercise for an indefinite period of time what Marx termed a "dictatorship of the proletariat." By this he apparently meant that the victorious working class could not permit the defeated class of big property owners, the bourgeoisie, to share in political power. Marx intended the workers' monopoly of political power to be temporary. He may have supposed that even during the period of proletarian dictatorship there could be more than one political party representing the interests of workers but advocating different public policies.

In reality the dictatorship of the proletariat has been very different from what Marx envisioned. Only one political party, the communist party, has been permitted to function. In some communist societies, the head of state has occupied that position until his death. Democratic liberties hard-won by human kind, such as freedom of the press and association, and the elements of due process, have not been tolerated.

What humanity decisively rejected in the year 1989 was communism as it had existed in nations associated with the Soviet Union.

Socialism, however, is not necessarily the same thing as communism. It is true that the Soviet Union and its allies described themselves as "socialist" countries, and this has been confusing. It is also true that socialist economic planning, even in societies that are politically democratic, has often been top-down, bureaucratic, and inefficient.

Nevertheless, leading spokespersons for socialism in the history of the United States presented socialism as a set of arrangements that would be more, not less, democratic than capitalism. Henry Demarest Lloyd, in his *Wealth Against Commonwealth*, said that America had done away with the undemocratic, one-man rule of kings, and now it needed to do away with the undemocratic, one-man rule of corporate executives. Eugene Debs compared the dependency of the wage worker in a capitalist economy to the human slavery abolished by the Civil War, and called capitalism "industrial slavery." Their proposition was that if it was right to elect political representatives, to hold them accountable, and to periodically replace them, we should also elect those whose economic decisions affect our lives.

The *Port Huron Statement*, by which the newly formed Students for a Democratic Society (SDS) announced its existence in 1962, although it did not use the word "socialism," criticized capitalism in the same way. "The anarchic actions of industrial leaders should become structurally responsible to the people," SDS declared. There should be "increased worker participation in decision-making." The nation required "experiments in decentralization" and a "proliferation" of public authorities like the Tennessee Valley Authority. In general, the *Port Huron Statement* espoused "participatory democracy," the notion that people should participate in the decisions that affect their lives. And like Henry Demarest Lloyd, like Eugene Debs, like Norman Thomas, SDS insisted that this should be just as true in our economic as in our political lives.

A long-time rank-and-file worker and labor editor, Stan Weir, puts this same thought in still another way. Why is it, he asks workers, that when a worker hits the time-clock he or she gives up the rights enjoyed as a citizen on the public sidewalk outside the plant? The Fourth Amendment states that a citizen may not be searched without a search warrant. Yet plant protection personnel consider themselves empowered to search lockers or personal belongings at will. Other amendments provide that if charged with a crime we are innocent until proven guilty and have a right to confront our accusers. Yet a foreman can send a worker home without due process of any kind, and the worker then faces the arduous burden of proving , through a never-ending grievance procedure or in court, that he or she was innocent. What does it say about our society that as workers we enjoy fewer rights than as citizens? Is there not a need to constitutionalize the workplace, so that the First, Fourth, and Fourteenth Amendments apply there, too?

In a nutshell: Socialism is the project of making economic institutions democratic. There is nothing wrong with this idea. It is a great idea. The problem is that socialists have not been sufficiently specific in describing a more democratic healthcare system (a system that would not leave more than thirty-five million Americans without medical insurance of any kind), a more democratic way of providing housing (so that there would no longer be millions of homeless persons seeking shelter), or a more democratic kind of steel company (such that profit-maximizing corporations could not throw away communities like Flint, Michigan, or Youngstown, Ohio, like so many orange peels).

There is a reason we have not been more specific.

During the transition from a feudal to a capitalist society, say from 1300 to 1800 AD, the process of change was fundamentally decentralized. Feudal societies were harsh, but they were loosely coordinated and small-scale, with a great deal of social space for the creation of new kinds of institutions. Artisans could form guilds. Merchants could organize free cities. Discontented serfs could run away to them. If you were a Protestant, you and a few friends could print your own Bible in the language of everyday life. If you were a scientist, you could drop stones from a leaning tower. The bourgeoisie did not initially need to seize state power. It could form corporations, and reconstruct the economy from within.

The task of incrementally transforming a capitalist economy seems to be much more difficult. Marxist rhetoric speaks of building "the new society within the shell of the old" or "the seed of the new society within the womb of the old," but the reality is otherwise. Assembly-line labor in a capitalist factory is, let us hope, not the prefiguration of anything in the future. Trade unions, as they exist in the United States—top-down, bureaucratic, inefficient institutions that mirror the capitalist corporations which they purport to challenge—are part of the problem, not part of the solution. Successful cooperative enterprises, or successful so-called "worker-owned" enterprises like Weirton Steel, succeed in the marketplace but do not transform the marketplace. There is a dearth of what Andre Gorz called revolutionary reforms, that is, small steps that point in a qualitatively new direction.

It is an historical irony that those revolutions in the twentieth century that have had the opportunity in the twentieth century to try to construct a new society within the shell of the old are guerrilla movements in Third World nations: Che Guevara starting health clinics as Cuban revolutionaries widened the liberated zone in the Sierra Mastre, Mao Zedong distributing land to those who tilled it in the revolutionary enclave of Yenan province. The irony is that these same movements, thus provided an opportunity to change things in an incremental, small-scale fashion, are the movements that ended in the very communist societies that the world has rejected.

What is to be done?

Henry David Thoreau writes somewhere that what each of us can communicate to others is his or her own personal experience. In this spirit, and not because I attribute special importance to happenings in my own life, I want to share what I have experienced for many recent years as a Legal Services lawyer. I consider that I have had the unusual opportunity to work in a place that gives one a glimpse of what a democratic, decentralized socialism might be like. Please do not suppose that I regard this institution as perfect. For example, Legal Services lawyers are forbidden to represent aliens, homosexuals, and persons with military problems, and to engage in training of labor organizers—restrictions every one of which seems unconstitutional to me.

Nonetheless, this is a remarkable institution, a model for how many other goods and services might be provided.

First, the Congress appropriates about $300 million a year for the provision of Legal Services throughout the United States. Pause on this point. There can be no development without capital, or in the language of the Mahoning Valley, there is no free lunch. The exciting, exhilarating, till-now unbelievable aspect of recent world history is that today, for the first time in my lifetime, one can speak plausibly and pragmatically of taking billions of dollars from the military budget, and using the money in other ways.

Second, while something like 95 percent of the money appropriated by Congress is distributed to field offices like the one I work for in Youngstown, it is channeled through a national public corporation, the National Legal Services Corporation. Pause here as well. Like the directors of the Tennessee Valley Authority, the directors of the National Legal Services Corporation are named by the national government. They are not much more accountable to the workers they hire or the customers they service than are the directors of IBM or U.S. Steel. TVA has been very much criticized for its lack of accountability to the grassroots. No doubt this criticism also applies to the National Legal Services Corporation, and especially so during the Reagan years, when President Reagan took away from Congress the selection of Legal Services directors (by making recess appointments) and appointed persons many of whom were out of sympathy with the entire Legal Services project, and, in the view of many, actively tried to destroy Legal Services.

Nevertheless, I believe that the national corporation has performed an indispensable function, even during the Reagan presidency. The corporation sends monitoring teams to each Legal Services field office every two or three years to inquire as to whether the office is acting consistently with the Legal Services statute and the regulations promulgated thereunder.

Understandably, field offices experience these visits with some apprehension. But are they not essential? How else would you ensure that local offices of a national institution were acting in conformity with the national purpose? If we hypothesize a field office of Legal Services that was running amok not in a Leftward direction, but in a Rightward one, for example assisting the Ku Klux Klan in unlawful activities, would we not wish that there exist a routinized way for the Congress to become aware of the fact? Like national funding, a national supervising administration seems to me an essential element of the Legal Services model.

A third element is the distribution of funds to Legal Services field offices on the basis of a mechanical formula, namely, the number of persons below the congressionally determined poverty guideline in the jurisdictions served by different offices. Obviously the use of such a formula helps to eliminate favoritism, political bias, and the like. Obviously, too, it might not be quite so easy for (let us say) a National Steel Corporation to decide which local areas were deserving of additional funds for their various steel mills. Rather than providing funds for legal services to both Youngstown and Marion, Ohio, on the basis of the number of poor persons in each, as the National Legal Services Corporation does, a national steel corporation might have to choose between Youngstown and Marion as the site for a new mill.

A fourth element in the Legal Services scheme is that each of the field offices is an independent entity administered by a board composed of workers, that is, lawyers, and consumers, that is, representatives of client organizations. Thus a Legal Services field office resembles a worker-community managed industrial enterprise, like the worker-community owned steel mills we have tried to set up in Youngstown. There is room for criticism. The lawyers on Legal Services boards are altogether lawyers from the community, and not lawyers who work for Legal Services, with the result that the latter have often formed unions so as to have a voice. But these are matters as to which there are legitimate grounds for difference, and a variety of experiments should be desired. The fundamental point is that Legal Services is not a faceless bureaucracy, is not run from Washington, but is decentralized and democratically managed.

Finally, Legal Services lawyers receive (modest) salaries and offer their services to eligible clients free of charge. This is the most important thing, perhaps. These days, as communism crumbles in Eastern Europe, we hear a great deal about market economies. But surely there must be a third alternative, on the one hand different from the command economy of communism, but on the other hand prepared to provide goods and services people need for some reason other than profit. I cannot think of a single good argument for offering health care, or legal services, on the basis of which cases will make most money for the service provider. Legal workers like my wife and myself who have worked in profit-maximizing law offices, and had our work measured by how much money we produced for the firm, experienced a liberation of our craftsmanship and of our best selves as human beings when we began to work for Legal Services. We can try to do what is needed by the human being before us rather than worrying about what that human being can pay, or how much the case is "worth" in dollars.

When I think about what socialism might look like, I think of my experience in Legal Services. Growing out of the neighborhood law offices of the Office of Economic Opportunity in the 1960s, Legal Services is one of the

relatively few impulses of the 1960s that has been institutionalized in lasting form. Nationally funded but locally
administered, it represents a third way between state socialism on the one hand, and dog-eat-dog market capitalism on
the other.

Summary

In describing new organizational forms—shopfloor committees, parallel central labor unions, nationally funded programs
administered by democratic local bodies made up of workers
and consumers—I am anxious not to be understood me-
chanically or over-literally. Labels are not important. The art
of this new kind of organizing is to discern where solidarity
unionism is beginning to happen, and to help it take shape
and sustain itself.

We must be ready to recognize new forms in many
guises. For instance, in Youngstown, Solidarity USA was a
parallel central labor body for retirees, and WATCH was a
central labor body for disabled workers. Thus there can be
more than one alterative central labor body: there can be
different entities, responding to different constituencies or
problems, but with the common feature of cutting across
workplace boundaries. Solidarity USA and WATCH recognized their kinship, met in the same hall, and fraternally
(and sororally) supported each other.

Although the forms described are essentially local, in
times of crisis shopfloor committees and parallel central labor
bodies will reach out to make contact with their counterparts

elsewhere. Polish Solidarity is a classic example. Another was the network of miners' committees in the Soviet Union, set up entirely outside the official trade unions, that succeeded in staging a nationwide strike in that immense country. Longshoremen in Spain, meatpackers and coal miners in the United States, have formed the same kind of networks. We don't need more proof of this phenomenon to know that it can happen.

Chapter Four

Our Union Makes Us Strong

According to the *Little Red Songbook* of the Industrial Workers of the World, the last verse of "Solidarity Forever" goes like this:

> In our hands is placed a power greater than their hoarded gold,
> Greater than the might of armies, magnified a thousandfold.
> We can bring to birth a new world from the ashes of the old,
> For the Union makes us strong.

We might ask ourselves, what does the last line of the song mean when it refers to "the Union." This song was sung in the 1930s by striking rubber workers, auto workers, and steel workers, who must have assumed that "the Union" meant their own, new CIO union: the URW, or the UAW, or the USWA. But that is almost certainly not what Ralph Chaplin, the Wobbly author of the song, had in mind.

The Union in "Solidarity Forever" is not today's industrial union, with its collective bargaining agreements and full-time staff. The Wobblies did not believe in collective bargaining agreements. They were highly skeptical of full-time staff. When they used the term "the Union" they meant the one big industrial union that included all the working people of the world. This is clear from other Wobbly songs. Thus in "Are You a Wobbly?" the chorus says: "Are you a Wobbly? . . . the One Big Union beckons to you"; and the second verse asserts:

> You like the idea, but then you say,
> "How can we do it—when is the day?"
> When all the poor folks, the unemployed folks
> And everyone who works for a wage
> Gets in the Union, One Union Grand . . .

"Amazing Boss," sung to the tune of "Amazing Grace," declares: "The time is now to organize, A Union of our class."

Joe Hill, the most famous Wobbly of them all, used the term "the Union" to mean the one big union of all workers. In "Workers of the World Awaken," he wrote:

> Join the Union, Fellow Workers
> Men and Women side by side . . .
> Unite ye slaves of ev'ry nation
> In One Union Grand.

And another Joe Hill song, "There Is Power in the Union," to the tune of "There Is Power in the Blood," contains these lines:

> There is pow'r, there is pow'r
> In a band of working folk,

When they stand hand in hand;
That's a pow'r, that's a pow'r
That must rule in every land:
One Industrial Union Grand.

The words "the Union makes us strong," therefore, simply mean, "our solidarity makes us strong." They mean solidarity unionism.

I want to say a few more words about the spirit in which we build solidarity unionism across boundaries of nation, gender, and religious faith.

For some time to come, the actions we may be able to take on behalf of a new kind of labor internationalism will be modest. We are at an early stage of organizing when what we are really doing is meeting people, making friends, building community in a one-on-one manner.

This means somehow finding the time and money physically to take ourselves to other countries. A Youngstown friend, John Barbero, used to use the thirteen-week vacation in the Steelworkers' contract to visit other steelworkers in the Soviet Union and Japan. Similarly, Stan Weir and Don Fitz went to Spain to come to know the Coordinadora movement on the Spanish docks. In 1988, eight of us from Youngstown, Aliquippa, and Pittsburgh (three steelworkers, a sheet metal worker, an electric lineman, a priest, and two lawyers) spent two weeks at a Nicaraguan steel mill.

And solidarity unionism is unionism in the spirit not only of the Wobblies and the rank-and-file organizers of the 1930s, of the civil rights movement of the early 1960s, and of our heroic brothers and sisters at Hormel and Pittston—solidarity unionism is also unionism recreated and rediscovered in the spirit of the feminist movement. One of the reasons why the labor movement is so dead, and so dull, is the degree to which it is dominated by males, and by masculine values of fighting, domination, and ranking people one above the other. Innovation is likely to come from the margins, from the unorganized, from the disregarded, and this means among other things that the new will often come from women, and be led by women. In Youngstown, the charismatic leader who founded Solidarity USA was a retiree's wife, and the first chairperson of WATCH was a woman, too. I believe we will find, as we come to meet our counterparts in other countries that very often the conveners of base communities and the spokespersons for shopfloor organizations—although less often those who go to international conferences— are women. We should cherish the feminization of the labor movement; we should recognize the kinship in spirit between feminism and solidarity; and those of us who are male should deliberately seek to step back from the role of spokesperson, and to learn to lead by serving.

For some of us, there is also a religious dimension to what we will be doing. The Pittston strikers acted out civil disobedience to a degree unknown in this country since the 1960s, and it is said that Cecil Roberts and other strike leaders were influenced by *The Parting of the Waters*, a biography of Martin Luther King written by Taylor Branch.

Indeed, according to Reverend Jim Sessions, who took part in the occupation of Pittston's Moss 3 coal preparation plant in September 1989, Roberts "has frequently been known to quote an entire passage of King's speeches from memory while his Appalachian audience listens in rapt attention."

The Pittston strike should cause us to reflect about violence and non-violence, and the religious roots of non-violent civil disobedience, because Appalachian coalfields like "bloody Harlan" and Mingo County have a history of no-holds-barred use of guns and dynamite against company goons and scabs. In Sessions's journal of the Moss 3 occupation, he states that the hundred miners who participated were selected (in part) on the basis of a personal commitment to non-violence. The unarmed occupiers advanced into the plant with their hands held above their heads to show that they had no weapons and under instructions that if shots were fired they were to kneel and wait for further orders. Outside Moss 3, among the thousands of supporters who gathered to protect the occupation, miners and their families knelt in prayer and sang "Amazing Grace" along with "Solidarity Forever." Inside the plant, Sessions was one of two ministers invited to say prayers each morning and as the miners stood in a circle before ending the occupation. One morning, he recalls, he asked "for silent prayers . . . for the casualties and sacrifices of all wars, including this one; I bid us to remember that all wars are in some ways class wars like this one."[1]

---

1. Jim Sessions and Fran Ansley, "Singing Across Dark Spaces: The Union/Community Takeover of the Pittston Coal Company's Moss 3 Coal Preparation Plant," in *Nonviolence in America: A Documentary*

We will find much the same thing as we come to know Latin American militants. In that part of the world, as in the Pittston strike, many persons experience labor solidarity and building "the Kingdom of God" as two ways of talking about the same thing.

There is a scene in the movie *Romero* that gathers into one image the spirit of solidarity across boundaries. A young Hispanic woman is taken to a garbage dump to be shot by a rightwing death squad. She is slight, black-haired. There is blood all over her white dress and she presumably has been repeatedly raped. Later we are told that her tongue has been cut out. She is directed to kneel. Instead, she remains standing, and tottering, turns to face those who are about to kill her.

She is from the Third World. She is a woman. A Christian who took religion seriously, she has become a revolutionary. I think she is saying to us that although we are few, and are just beginning, and feel overwhelmed by the forces arrayed against us, nothing on earth can prevent our union—our solidarity—from prevailing in the end.

History, revised edition, eds. Staughton Lynd and Alice Lynd (Maryknoll, NY: Orbis Books, 1995), pp. 374–96.

Appendix

Extracts from
We Are the Union
by Ed Mann

I BELIEVE IN DIRECT ACTION

I THINK WE'VE GOT TOO MUCH CONTRACT. YOU HATE TO BE
the guy who talks about the good old days, but I think the
IWW had a darn good idea when they said, "Well, we'll
settle these things as they arise."

I believe in direct action. Once a problem is put on paper and gets into the grievance procedure, you might as well
kiss that paper goodbye. When the corporations started recognizing unions, they saw this. They co-opted the unions
with the grievance procedure and the dues check-off. They
quit dealing with the rank and file and started dealing with
people who wanted to be bosses like them, the union bosses.

We were the troublemakers. We'd have a wildcat strike.
The international would say, "Either you get back to work
or you're fired." It wasn't the company saying this. It was the
union.

The Dolomite Gun and the Bonus System

One strike we led, they had a dolomite gun they used to spray the furnaces after the heat was tapped out. Prior to them getting this piece of equipment we used to have to shovel in the dolomite. It was in the summertime and the superintendent wouldn't use the gun. It was real hot. So we just stayed on the floor or went to the office and said, "We're not going to do any shoveling until you put that gun on the floor to give us some relief." We got help like that. Most of the superintendents in that time had come up through the ranks and they knew the conditions of the job. They knew you weren't kidding.

But in a production department, say like where Archie Nelson was where people were scarfing, if they slowed down it affected production. Sometimes the stuff was needed at the next point of operations on a certain timetable. The further a piece of metal gets down through the operation, the more costly it becomes. So the further down the line you make your move or your action, it becomes more costly to the company. If you're at the finish where they are going to ship the pipe and you refuse to load it, because it's gone through all these steps that piece of pipe is worth X number of dollars where when it was in the furnace as molten metal it was worth only pennies.

In the Open Hearth, you worked on a big furnace that held two hundred tons of molten metal. If you slowed down the operation, you'd burn the furnace up. The furnace would melt. And then you had a lot of physical hard work repairing the furnace, shoveling and so on: backbreaking work. The idea was to get the heat out as quick as you could; make your steel; get it out of the furnace so it wouldn't tear the furnace up and you made a little bit of bonus.

The people who could slow down the procedure were the people who charged the furnaces, who put in the scrap and molten iron. These were the charging machine men and cranemen. They had a little control over how the operation went. If your first helper wanted two boxes of raw lime and a box of ore in the furnace to make the steel up to specifications, the charging machine man could give them a little extra or not enough and screw up everything.

The longer you keep molten steel in a furnace the more likely you are to tear up the production equipment. You tap the steel into a ladle. You got to get it out of that ladle and into the molds or it's going to freeze up on the ladle. We're talking about two hundred tons of steel in one big chunk. There's the labor of putting new brick in and of the boiler-maker doing patchwork. And if you don't get the steel to the blooming mill in a certain period of time it's going to get too cold and they will have to reheat it, which costs money, and it will change the make-up of the steel. You got to hit them where it hurts.

Once they were going to change the bonus system. They were going to give the first helper and the second helper an increase in bonus and cut the third helpers. In other words, they were just moving the money around. Third helpers refused to go out on the job. Second helpers stuck with them. Then there was nobody out there to help the first helpers so they agreed to go out with us. It was a wildcat.

Well, we were out that night. The midnight turn comes out and finds out about this. We are all sitting in the wash-room. The company comes out with the president of the local, Danny Thomas.

"What's the problem here?" There's the plant manager and the local union president and so on.

I'm sitting there. As spokesman for the group I said, "They're cutting our bonus. We don't want to hear it."

Danny Thomas says to the superintendent, "You get rid of that guy and your troubles are over." And the whole Open Hearth gang is sitting there. This doesn't hurt me politically at all. It got the guys hotter. They didn't care about getting rid of me. They didn't want to lose our bonus!

The superintendent was crying, "What am I going to do with this steel?" I said, "Tap it out on the ground. I don't care what you do with it."

He said, "The blast furnace is ready to tap. We got to move that iron."

"Dump it on the ground," I said. "We want our bonus."

They agreed.

"Now who's going to get paid? Are we going to get paid for the time we've been docked here?"

"Oh, we can't do that. You guys didn't do any work."

We said, "The furnace did the work. We want paid or we're going home right now." And it worked.

"You wonder why Danny Thomas and I didn't get along? He tells the superintendent that if he gets rid of me his troubles are over."

THE WILDCAT OVER TONY'S DEATH

This was the first experience I had that showed that *people* can really be involved. At the time I was Recording Secretary of the local, and John [Barbero] and I were both stewards in the Open Hearth. We filed a grievance with the superintendent about 33 different safety violations. One of the items was we wanted vehicles to have back-up signals. They used big heavy trucks in the pit. There was a lot of noise. It was hard to hear. We wanted a warning horn on the back so when a truck was going to back up the people working there could hear it.

The company rejected the grievance out of hand. They weren't going to discuss any of the 33 demands.

Shortly after the grievance was rejected, a man who was going to retire in about seven days was run over by one of these trucks. He was crushed. He was a well-liked person who had worked there a long time and was about to retire. This happened on day turn, about one o'clock in the afternoon.

I was working afternoon turn that day, three to eleven. I came out to work and somebody said, "Tony got killed." "How did he get killed?" "You remember that grievance you filed asking for back-up signals on the truck? The truck backed over him and crushed him."

So I got up on the bench in the washroom and I say to the guys coming to work, "What are we going to do about this? Are we going to work under these lousy conditions? Who's next? Who's going to get killed next? Don't we give a damn about Tony?" The guys agreed to go out.

Now some didn't agree to go out. "What's the matter with you guys? Here you are. A union brother murdered. We had a grievance in and it was rejected. Are you going to let the company pull this shit?" We actually had to drag some people out because we had all kinds of people. "That's not my problem. I don't work down there. I run a crane." "Let's get out! Let's go!"

We went up to the union hall. We were the afternoon turn that was supposed to go to work. Day turn was finished working, they've tapped the heats out, and the people working the day turn now come up to the union hall. We've got two turns there. We tell them the situation. They agree, "Shut her down!" The guys called their buddies on the midnight turn from the union hall. "Don't come out to work tonight."

John was out of town that weekend. They were looking to me for leadership. I said, "Here's what we'll do. Rather than get the stewards fired, let's appoint a committee for each area and let's start listing our demands on safety," bypassing the union structure. It worked. Every area—pit, cranes, floor—was represented.

In the meantime Lefty DeLarco, who was departmental chairman of the open hearth at that time, was working day turn. He calls over to the union hall on the company phone and says, "Hey Ed, what's going on? Why aren't these guys coming to work?" I'm sure the phone is bugged. I could have been fired for leading the strike. I say, "Why don't you come up here, Lefty, and find out?"

The company called the international union rep. "What's going on here?" "There's nothing going on until these grievances are resolved." "What grievances?" We didn't just say, "Goddamn it, Tony got killed and we're shutting it down." We said, "This is what we want. Get a meeting with the company. We'll meet at any time they want."

They set up a meeting for that night, about nine o'clock. They had to get the plant manager from wherever he was. The company said, "We're only going to deal with the departmental chairmen." I said, "Then you're not going to deal with anybody because this is the committee." I said, "The only reason you want to deal with Lefty is you want to fire him," which wasn't the case but it got Lefty off the hook. He wouldn't have to tell the people to go back to work.

We refused even to have the superintendent in the office because it was he who rejected the grievance. We said, "We're not going to deal with him if he can't answer. We want to talk to somebody that has more authority." They brought in the division manager. We met late in the night with the company and all the next day.

They agreed to everything. They wanted this committee to meet with the company on a regular basis on safety conditions, bypassing the safety committee because this was an immediate issue, whereas the safety committee worked on things month by month—a meeting this month to correct a light bulb burned out, next month they come back and say, we don't have any light bulbs.

So next day we have a meeting at the union hall to explain what happened, what we gained and all that. We're discussing whether we're going back to work or not and I'm saying to the guys, "Look, if there's anything else you want, let's hear it." Then the Youngstown newspaper comes out. It reports the accident and the strike and it says, "Tony got killed because of his own negligence." The company sent out that statement. The guys got furious. "We want that statement retracted in tomorrow's paper." Not just a phone call or a letter. They wanted it in the paper, retracted. The paper doesn't come out for another 24 hours. The guys stayed out another day. And in the next day's paper they retracted that statement and the guys went back to work.

They reprimanded everybody in the Open Hearth that went out and they gave me three days off. We said, "Wait a minute, take the reprimands away." And they did take them off everybody else. I said, "Hey, I don't care. You guys go back to work."

Other departments didn't go out in sympathy, but there was just no work for them. We made the steel. Everything cost, measured as trainloads of material coming in or scrap half loaded. That's a feeling of power. And it isn't something you're doing as an individual. You're doing it as a group.

If you're not going to *do* something, then you're not going to be a leader, are you? I had credibility. I'd just gotten elected Recording Secretary. I got more votes out of the Open Hearth than the president got. The grievance was rejected. The guy was going to retire. It was an emotional issue. He was a guy everybody liked. It wasn't prepared timing. It fell into place. You've got to recognize those situations. Be there when there are credible steps to take. Some people, it never happens in their lives. I was lucky.

A Note on Staughton Lynd

STAUGHTON LYND HAS BEEN A LONG-DISTANCE RUNNER IN the movement for fundamental social change. In the late 1950s he joined the group that produced *Liberation* magazine. From 1961 to 1964 he taught history at Spelman College in Atlanta, a college for black women. In the summer of 1964 he directed the Freedom Schools of the Mississippi Summer Project. When the war in Vietnam escalated, in April 1965 Staughton Lynd served as chairperson of the first march on Washington against the war; and in December 1965 he made a controversial fact-finding trip to Hanoi with Tom Hayden and Herbert Aptheker.

Staughton and his wife, Alice Lynd, began working in and for the rank-and-file labor movement in the late 1960s. They collected oral histories of men and women active in creating the CIO and published them in a book called *Rank and File*, now available in an expanded edition from Haymarket Books. Three of the interviews in the book inspired the movie *Union Maids*.

The Lynds have been lawyers as well as historians. Until their retirement in 1996, they worked on employment cases at a legal services office in Youngstown, Ohio, providing free representation in civil matters to persons who could not afford a private lawyer. Staughton Lynd represented a coalition of local unions, individual workers, and community groups that sought to prevent Youngstown's steel mills from closing or to reopen the mills under worker-community ownership. He describes the struggle in *The Fight Against Shutdowns* (Singlejack Books, 1982).

Other publications on the labor movement by Staughton Lynd include *"We Are All Leaders": The Alternative Unionism of the Early 1930s*, essays edited by Staughton (University of Illinois Press, 1996); *The New Rank and File*, additional oral histories edited by Staughton and Alice (Cornell University, 2000); *Labor Law for the Rank and Filer: Building Solidarity While Staying Clear of the Law*, Staughton Lynd with Daniel Gross (PM Press, 2011); *Solidarity Unionism at Starbucks*, Staughton with Daniel Gross (PM Press, 2011); and Staughton Lynd, *Doing History from the Bottom Up: On E.P. Thompson, Howard Zinn, and Rebuilding the Labor Movement from Below* (Haymarket Books, 2014).

A Note on Mike Konopacki

MIKE KONOPACKI IS A POLITICAL CARTOONIST FROM Wisconsin, specializing in labor issues. He is co-author and illustrator of Howard Zinn's graphic history *A People's History of American Empire*.

A Note on Immanuel Ness

IMMANUEL NESS IS A POLITICAL ECONOMIST WHO specializes in labor unions and professor of political science at City University of New York. He is editor of *WorkingUSA: The Journal of Labor and Society* and author of numerous works including *New Forms of Worker Organization* (PM Press). He was a worker and union organizer in the food, maintenance, and publishing industries.

Index

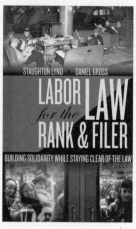

LABOR LAW FOR THE RANK AND FILER
BUILDING SOLIDARITY WHILE STAYING CLEAR OF THE LAW (2ND EDITION)
Staughton Lynd and Daniel Gross
$12.00 • 8x5 • 120 Pages

Labor Law for the Rank and Filer is a guerrilla legal handbook for workers in a precarious global economy. Blending cutting-edge legal strategies for winning justice at work with a theory of dramatic social change from below, it delivers a practical guide for making work better while re-invigorating the labor movement.

Labor Law for the Rank and Filer demonstrates how a powerful model of organizing called "Solidarity Unionism" can help workers avoid the pitfalls of the legal system and utilize direct action to win. This new revised and expanded edition includes new cases governing fundamental labor rights as well as an added section on Practicing Solidarity Unionism. This new section discusses the hard-hitting tactic of working to rule; organizing under the principle that no one is illegal, and building grassroots solidarity across borders to challenge neoliberalism, among several other new topics.

SOLIDARITY UNIONISM AT STARBUCKS
Staughton Lynd and Daniel Gross with illustrations by Tom Keough
$4.95 • 8.5x5.5 • 36 Pages

Utilizing the principles of solidarity unionism, any group of co-workers can start building an organization to win an independent voice at work without waiting for a traditional trade union to come and "organize" them. Indeed, in a leaked recording of a conference call, the nation's most prominent union-busting lobbyist coined a term, "the Starbucks problem," as a warning to business executives about the risk of working people organizing themselves and taking direct action to improve issues at work.

New Forms of Worker Organization
The Syndicalist and Autonomist Restoration of Class Struggle Unionism
Edited by Immanuel Ness
Foreword by Staughton Lynd
$24.95 • 9x6 • 336 Pages

As unions implode and weaken, workers are independently forming their own unions, drawing on the tradition of syndicalism and autonomism—a resurgence of self-directed action that augurs a new period of class struggle throughout the world. Workers worldwide are rejecting leaders and forming authentic class-struggle unions rooted in sabotage, direct action, and striking to achieve concrete gains.

The tangible evidence marshaled in this book serves as a guide for understanding the obstacles and opportunities for workers challenging neoliberal capitalism, even as the unions of the old decline and disappear.

Contributors: Au Loong-Yu, Bai Ruixue, Shawn Hattingh, Piotr Bizyukov and Irina Olimpieva, Genese M. Sodikoff, Aviva Chomsky, Dario Bursztyn, Gabriel Kuhn, Erik Forman, Steven Manicastri, Arup Kumar Sen, Verity Burgmann, Ray Jureidini, Meredith Burgmann, and Jack Kirkpatrick.

Accompanying
Pathways to Social Change
Staughton Lynd
$14.95 • 8 x5 • 176 Pages

In *Accompanying*, Staughton Lynd distinguishes two strategies of social change. The first, characteristic of the 1960s Movement in the United States, is "organizing." The second, articulated by Archbishop Oscar Romero of El Salvador, is "accompaniment." The critical difference is that in accompanying one another the promoter of social change and his or her oppressed colleague view themselves as two experts, each bringing indispensable experience to a shared project. Together, as equals, they seek to create what the Zapatistas call "another world."

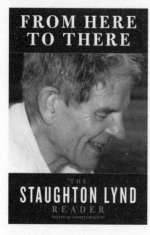

FROM HERE TO THERE
THE STAUGHTON LYND READER
Staughton Lynd • Edited with an Introduction by Andrej Grubacic
$22.00 • 9x6 • 320 Pages

From Here To There is both a definitive introduction and further exploration, bound to educate, enlighten, and inspire. In a wide-ranging Introduction, anarchist scholar Andrej Grubacic considers how Lynd's persistent concerns relate to traditional anarchism.

The first section of the *Reader* collects reminiscences and analyses of the 1960s. A second section offers a vision of how historians might immerse themselves in popular movements while maintaining their obligation to tell the truth. In the last section Lynd explores what nonviolence, resistance to empire as a way of life, and working class self-activity might mean in the 21st century. Together, they provide a sweeping overview of the life, and work—to date—of Staughton Lynd.

WOBBLIES AND ZAPATISTAS
CONVERSATIONS ON ANARCHISM, MARXISM AND RADICAL HISTORY
Staughton Lynd and Andrej Grubacic
$20.00 • 8x5 • 300 Pages

Wobblies and Zapatistas offers an encounter between two generations and traditions. Andrej Grubacic is an anarchist from the Balkans. Staughton Lynd is a lifelong pacifist, influenced by Marxism. They meet in dialogue in an effort to bring together the anarchist and Marxist traditions, to discuss the writing of history by those who make it, and to remind us of the idea that "my country is the world." Encompassing a Left-libertarian perspective and an emphatically activist standpoint, these conversations are meant to be read in the clubs and affinity groups of the new Movement.

About
PM Press

PM Press was founded at the end of 2007 by a small collection of folks with decades of publishing, media, and organizing experience. PM Press co-conspirators have published and distributed hundreds of books, pamphlets, CDs, and DVDs. Members of PM have founded enduring book fairs, spearheaded victorious tenant organizing campaigns, and worked closely with bookstores, academic conferences, and even rock bands to deliver political and challenging ideas to all walks of life. We're old enough to know what we're doing and young enough to know what's at stake.

We seek to create radical and stimulating fiction and nonfiction books, pamphlets, T-shirts, visual and audio materials to entertain, educate, and inspire you. We aim to distribute these through every available channel with every available technology, whether that means you are seeing anarchist classics at our bookfair stalls; reading our latest vegan cookbook at the café; downloading geeky fiction e-books; or digging new music and timely videos from our website.

Contact us for direct ordering and questions about all PM Press releases, as well as manuscript submissions, review copy requests, foreign rights sales, author interviews, to book an author for an event, and to have PM Press attend your bookfair:

PM Press • PO Box 23912 • Oakland, CA 94623

510-658-3906 • info@pmpress.org

Buy books and stay on top of what we are doing at:

www.pmpress.org

FOPM

These are indisputably momentous times—the financial system is melting down globally and the Empire is stumbling. Now more than ever there is a vital need for radical ideas.

In the seven years since its founding—and on a mere shoestring—PM Press has risen to the formidable challenge of publishing and distributing knowledge and entertainment for the struggles ahead. With over 300 releases to date, we have published an impressive and stimulating array of literature, art, music, politics, and culture. Using every available medium, we've succeeded in connecting those hungry for ideas and information to those putting them into practice.

Friends of PM allows you to directly help impact, amplify, and revitalize the discourse and actions of radical writers, filmmakers, and artists. It provides us with a stable foundation from which we can build upon our early successes and provides a much-needed subsidy for the materials that can't necessarily pay their own way. You can help make that happen—and receive every new title automatically delivered to your door once a month—by joining as a Friend of PM Press. And, we'll throw in a free T-Shirt when you sign up.

Here are your options:
- $30 a month: Get all books and pamphlets plus 50% discount on all webstore purchases
- $40 a month: Get all PM Press releases (including CDs and DVDs) plus 50% discount on all webstore purchases
- $100 a month: Superstar—Everything plus PM merchandise, free downloads, and 50% discount on all webstore purchases

For those who can't afford $30 or more a month, we're introducing *Sustainer Rates* at $15, $10 and $5. Sustainers get a free PM Press t-shirt and a 50% discount on all purchases from our website.

Your Visa or Mastercard will be billed once a month, until you tell us to stop. Or until our efforts succeed in bringing the revolution around. Or the financial meltdown of Capital makes plastic redundant. Whichever comes first.